Teaching the Spoken Language

An approach based on
the analysis of
conversational English

*Gillian Brown and
George Yule*

CAMBRIDGE
UNIVERSITY PRESS

Published by the Press Syndicate of the University of Cambridge
The Pitt Building, Trumpington Street, Cambridge CB2 1RP
40 West 20th Street, New York, NY 10011–4211, USA
10 Stamford Road, Oakleigh, Melbourne 3166, Australia

© Cambridge University Press 1983

First published 1983
Eighth printing 1993

Printed and bound in Great Britain
at The Bath Press, Avon

Library of Congress catalogue card number: 83 – 15349

British Library cataloguing in publication data

Brown, Gillian

Teaching the spoken language.
1. English language – Spoken language – Study and
teaching
I. Title   II. Yule, George
428.3'07   PE1011

ISBN 0 521 25377 2 hard covers
ISBN 0 521 27384 6 paperback
ISBN 0 521 25378 0 cassette

Contents

Contents

Acknowledgements

Some of the data we cite here and some of the research findings which we discuss derive from a series of research projects, spread over nine years, supported by the Social Science Research Council and the Scottish Education Department. We are grateful to these bodies for support and to our fellow researchers, Anne H. Anderson, Roger Brown, Karen Currie de Carvalho, Joanne Kenworthy and Hilary Smith.

Many colleagues and former colleagues and students of the Department of Linguistics of Edinburgh University have contributed to the approach to spoken language which we present here. We are particularly indebted to David Abercrombie, Keith Brown, Pit Corder, Clive Criper, the late Julian Dakin, Alan Davies, Tony Howatt, Laurie Iles, the late Bill Jones, John Laver, Keith Mitchell, Ramsey Rutherford, Hugh Trappes-Lomax, Elizabeth Uldall and Henry Widdowson. In addition, we have learned a lot from friends and colleagues in other universities, particularly from Gerda Platzek and Jacqueline Schlissinger. We are immensely grateful to them all. Some of them may find it hard to discern traces of their contribution here and may well wish to disclaim any connection with statements which we make. Naturally we alone are responsible for the opinions expressed here.

We are grateful for technical assistance provided by Jeff Dodds, Cameron McMillan, Stewart Smith and Stan Stephen, to high school students, undergraduates (particularly Rachel Bell and Sarah Brown), and to innumerable others who have contributed to our collection of spoken language data and finally to Marion Law and Ethel Jack for typing the manuscript.

Preface

This book arises from a long-term concern with the teaching of the spoken language. In particular we are concerned with ways in which the spoken language differs from written language, and with how genres of spoken language differ from each other. We have restricted our discussion in this book in various ways. We rarely mention questions of pronunciation or intonation, which have so dominated the teaching of spoken language in the past. Nor do we discuss social variation within language. Nor do we discuss the teaching of grammar and vocabulary. These topics are clearly relevant to the teaching of spoken language and we ignore them only because so much has already been written about these areas. We have chosen to concentrate on the communicative use of language by speakers, with a reason for speaking, to listeners, in contexts. This leads us to a view of the spoken language which owes a great deal in its approach to the rapidly developing study of the analysis of discourse.

Some of the suggestions in this book are reasonably securely based, since they have been tested in use. This is particularly true of the sections on the teaching and assessment of spoken language production. Other parts are based on common sense, extrapolation from our own experience, as well as on the experience of many friends and colleagues who have contributed crucially to the approach we outline here. Occasionally we make suggestions on the basis of intuition, or some long-held but only partially-argued conviction. This avowal ought to be sufficient to warn the reader that he ought to scrutinise everything we claim in the light of his own experience and of the needs of his own students. It cannot be the case, in a general book of this kind, that everything is relevant to everybody.

We are particularly anxious that no teacher should see any of our proposals as attacking anything that he is doing at the moment. If it works for him, and for his students, he should almost certainly keep on doing it. Our hope is that we may add to the armoury of strategies and tools which every teacher needs to keep on adding to. If we are able to suggest anything at all that you haven't already thought of, try it out and see if it works. If it does work, make a bit of room for it in your curriculum. There are no inspirational, global, solutions here.

Data: recorded material and transcripts

One of our aims in this book is to draw to the attention, particularly of those who have not studied naturally occurring spoken language, the many differences between spoken language and written language. There are frequent quoted extracts of naturally occurring speech. These appear as transcriptions. All of the transcriptions, except for a few in chapter 4, are of native speakers of English, speaking naturally and spontaneously. The transcriptions are numbered in sequence in the chapter in which they occur. Some of the extracts are also exemplified on the accompanying cassette. In this case a second number appears in the text, following the chapter-sequence number. This second number indicates the taped extract number as it appears on the cassette. The same extract on the cassette is sometimes referred to, for different exemplificatory purposes, in different chapters.

The cassette is intended simply as an illustration of what we are talking about at a given point. It is not intended as a 'teaching' tape. Some of the extracts were recorded in noisy school environments, some in speakers' homes, so the quality is variable. Since in all cases the language is transcribed, we believe it is possible to discern the relevant material on the tape as we draw attention to it. Despite the variable quality, it seemed to us worthwhile to try to produce genuine material which we have used for teaching and assessment. Since we work in Scotland, there is naturally a preponderance of Scottish voices on the tape, though there are also RP speakers, American speakers, and speakers of other accents, as well as non-native speakers of English. The points illustrated by these voices are not, however, limited to particular accents or dialects, as the reader may quickly establish by listening to any native English speakers talking.

Each transcribed extract is presented in normal orthography. The detail presented in the transcription (particularly detail which is difficult to interpret) may vary from one discussion to the next, since particular transcriptions are presented for different purposes. We have transcribed words and pauses *as we hear them*. It is perfectly possible that an attentive listener may produce a different version if he undertook a detailed transcription. This should not occasion concern, but merely draw attention to the fact that there *are* often different possible interpretations of the blurred acoustic signal.

Pauses are represented thus: − a very brief pause
+ a short pause
++ a long pause

Overlapping between speakers is represented between vertical lines: | |

Omitted portions are represented by: . . .

Unclear parts which we have guessed are represented by: (?).

Parts where the speaker fails to fill in are represented by: * * *

1 The spoken language

1.0 Preliminaries

In this chapter we shall explore some of the differences in form and in function between spoken and written language. We shall point out that, within spoken language, certain distinctions need to be drawn, because they have an effect on the forms of language which are produced. The bulk of the chapter is devoted to considering the uses to which spoken language is put by native speakers of English, with extensive transcribed illustrations of this use. In the last sections we consider the implications of research findings about the behaviour of native speakers for the teaching of the spoken language to foreign learners.

1.1 Spoken and written language

For most of its history, language teaching has been concerned with the study of the written language. The written language is the language of literature and of scholarship. It is language which is admired, studied, and rich in excellent exemplification. Any well-educated person ought to have access to literature and scholarship in the language he is acquiring. The obvious procedure, it must follow, is to teach him the language through the excellent written models which can be selected and ordered by his teacher.

While the student is acquiring an understanding of the written language of these splendid models on the one hand, on the other he is himself practising the art of producing sentences of the language. An obvious advantage of the written language is that it has been described by generations of grammar-writers and dictionary-makers. There is a comforting sense in which it is possible to say that a written sentence is correct or not. The rules of writing English sentences are really rather well known and well described. Furthermore, written language does not vary greatly over a couple of centuries, and it does not vary very much depending on where it is written. Texts selected for foreign students to study were nearly all written in the nineteenth and twentieth centuries and are selected from writers who wrote standard English. Even American writers only deviate from this standard in relatively trivial ways, which can always be presented to the student in a 'corrected' form.

The serious consideration of the spoken language as a subject for teaching has a long history, but only made a decisive impact on foreign language teaching in general after the end of the Second World War. Initially major attention was devoted to the teaching of pronunciation. Students of the spoken language spent many hours learning to pronounce the 'sounds of English', first of all in isolation, then in short isolated words, and finally in short isolated sentences like:

(1.1)   – We'll have tea for three, please, for Jean, Steve, and me
             (practising i)
          – Pretty little Mrs Smith lives in the vicinity
             (practising ɪ)

Students spent hours in language lab booths listening to, and repeating, the vowels and consonants of English. Later on, stress patterns were added and, eventually, practice in intonation patterns. It is still possible to visit parts of the world where 'teaching the spoken language' is largely conceived of as teaching students to pronounce written sentences.

During the last twenty-five years, horizons for most foreign language teachers have widened. Students are not only taught to pronounce, but they are given practice in listening to, examples of carefully spoken English. They are required to discriminate between sounds or words spoken in isolation (a task which many native speakers have problems with). They are required to identify stressed words in taped sentences read aloud. In some cases they are required to identify intonation nuclei (or 'tonics') in short texts read aloud. Even more dramatically, many courses have abandoned using written texts read aloud, and have begun to use extracts from texts of 'real', 'authentic' conversations, radio broadcasts, lectures, etc. With the breaking out of the written mode, students are encouraged to use spoken-language forms spontaneously, not simply to utter 'written-language sentences'.

This expansion must obviously be welcomed because it provides, for many students, the ability to talk and listen in a foreign language, to communicate with speakers of the foreign language. In theory, at any rate, that's what it provides. For the teachers it often provides a real headache. Dozens of practical problems, which could be ignored when the subject-matter being taught was the written language, suddenly surface when the subject matter is the spoken language.

There is no longer a secure, tried-and-tested, teaching tradition to lean upon.

What is the appropriate form of spoken language to teach? From the point of view of pronunciation, what is a reasonable model? How important is pronunciation? Is it any more important than teaching appropriate handwriting in the foreign language? If so, why? From the point of view of the structures taught, is it all right to teach the spoken language as if it were exactly like the written language, but with a few 'spoken expressions' thrown in? Is it appropriate to teach the same structures to all foreign language students, no matter what their age is or their intentions in learning the spoken language? Are those structures which are described in standard grammars (like Quirk et al., 1972) the structures which our students should be expected to produce when they speak English? How is it possible to give students any sort of meaningful practice in producing spoken English? If you are teaching a class of twenty or more adolescents at a time, surely it must be obvious that a student will only receive sporadic practice in producing the spoken language as he answers the teacher's questions (except in the language lab which only permits the student to produce a limited answer to a limited question). Don't we have to accept that we are doing all we can?

From the point of view of listening comprehension, what is there that's different about written language from spoken language? Is it all right to play the student a tape and then ask him to answer multiple-choice questions on the content of what he has heard? How are materials for listening comprehension to be selected? Is there any way to grade them? What is the teacher to do about the incompleteness and frequent ungrammaticality of spontaneous native speech? Pretend it doesn't exist? Bend the rules for native speakers – talk about 'performance variability'? Is it reasonable anyway to bother to use 'authentic' materials when invented dialogues read aloud can be made so much more interesting, witty, clear, and correct?

The list of problems stretches on and on, and for many conscientious teachers the demands of teaching the spoken language are really worrying and put the teacher in a disadvantageous position. There is, to begin with, no influential description of spoken English which has, say, the status of grammars of written English. Spoken English appears very variable, and is very different from one dialect area to another. Even between speakers who mostly speak 'standard English' there is a different emphasis in their selection from forms in standard English. So, for example, many educated Scots, like many educated southern English speakers, will use all of the forms *I shall* / *I will*, and the relative pronouns *that* and *which*, but the Scottish speaker will use more of the forms *I will* and *that*, whereas the southern English speaker will use more of the forms *I shall* and *which*. Are these local differences worth commenting on?

Even more obviously, what is the status of the difference between the sort of speech produced by young members of the British speech community and that produced by adults, especially highly educated adults who spend their lives immersed in written language? The adults' speech may frequently have a great deal in common with the written language – hardly surprising, since they spend so much of their time reading it and writing it. If you only listen to speech produced by these people, as they are speaking fluently and confidently, on matters they have expressed themselves on many times before (like the speaker in extract (*1*) on the tape), it would be very reasonable of you to suppose that teaching the spoken language does indeed only mean teaching the student to speak the written language together with a few characteristic spoken phrases. If, however, you were to study the detail of the language of most of the rest of the speakers on our tape, which includes speech by educated adult speakers, undergraduate students and other highly intelligent members of the population, you would find that the transcripts of what they say do not strongly resemble written language in all particulars. It is obviously the case that the vast majority of the speakers of English are not highly educated, written-language immersed. Most speakers of English produce spoken language which is syntactically very much simpler than written language. The vocabulary is usually much less specific. Highly literate speakers may produce utterances with complex syntactic structures, a good deal of subordination and a confident marking-out of what they are going to say by phrases like *in the first place*, *in the second place* and *finally*. This is particularly common when speakers are reproducing expressions of opinion which they have thought a lot about, mentally 'rehearsed', or uttered on previous occasions. Most spoken language is not structured like this. Most spoken language consists of paratactic (unsubordinated) phrases which are marked as related to each other, not so much by the syntax as by the way the speaker says them. The speaker uses the resources of pausing and rhythm and, to a lesser extent, intonation, to mark out for the listener which parts of his speech need to be co-interpreted. Of course, what syntax there is will contribute to this structuring, but it is frequently the case that the syntax is rather simple. Consider extract (1.1). There is a certain amount of subordination in this extract, all introduced by simple common clause conjunctions *so, when, and, then, but, because*.

(1.2) (1)   D: on occasion we do a bit proof reading along there +
            K: uhuh
            D: and we're all sort of called on to do that from time to
               time
            K: what does that involve
            D: well + one of our main jobs in the Botanics is writing
               for the flora of Turkey +
            K: uhuh
            D: they haven't got the scientists to do it so + we sort of
               supply the scientists for that +
            K: uhuh
            D: well when + you've got all the scientific work written
               up + we all sort of check through it and one – reads
               and the others +
            K: oh I see you read aloud
            D: uhuh that's right
            K: I see
            D: and then you sort of switch back and forward like
               this +
            K: uhuh + and that doesn't bother you
            D: it does actually (laughter) I'm terrible at it + but I don't
               know
            K: even when it's something you're interested in +
            D: well it makes it a bit easier to read certainly but + em
               just because you're reading to somebody else you
               feel + a bit uneasy somehow
            K: uhuh
            J: I think it comes from + having to stand up and read in
               school +

The speakers here are all graduates, professional academics. The
main speaker, D, was due to give his first lecture the following week.
Despite the fact that these young adults spend their working lives
immersed in the written language, the spoken language they produce
here is relatively simple. D's first two remarks consist of simple
clause structures. He next remarks:

> well + one of our main jobs in the Botanics is writing for
> the flora of Turkey + they haven't got the (uhuh) scientists
> to do it

His second statement simply follows the first, and the listener has to
work out the relationship between them, how the second statement
relates to the first. In the written language, where sentences are
frequently more complex, it would be quite likely that a writer would
have inserted *because* before the second statement, thus explicitly
subordinating the explanatory statement to the first one. Consider
now D's remark:

> well when + you've got all the scientific work written up +
> we all sort of check through it and one – one reads and the
> others +

Here there is an explicitly marked temporal subordinate clause,
when. . ., but then note the simple addition of *we all sort of check it
through and one reads* which a writer of expository prose (this same
speaker in another role) would probably feel obliged to impose some
more structure on.

Notice, too, in the extract the 'incomplete sentences' which are
such a typical feature of spoken language:

> – and one – one reads and the others
> – and that doesn't bother you
> – but I don't know
> – even when it's something you're interested in

Observe, as well, the use of general non-specific words and phrases
which, again, are typical of spoken language:

> – *they* haven't *got* the scientists to *do it*
> – so we *sort of* supply the scientists for *that*
> – we all *sort of* check through it
> – and *one* reads and *the others*
> – *that's right*
> – *like this*
> – *and that doesn't bother you*
> – *it does actually*
> – even when it's *something*
> – *a bit* easier
> – *to somebody else*
> – *somehow*

The combination of loosely organised syntax, the number of general
non-specific words and phrases, the use of interactive expressions
like *well, oh, uhuh,* all contribute to the general impression that
information is packed very much less densely in spoken language of
this sort than it is, say, in expository prose like the prose you're
reading at the moment. Notice how relatively little information is
provided in each of the information-bearing chunks:

> – one of our main jobs in the Botanics is writing for the
>   flora of Turkey
> – they haven't got the scientists to do it
> – so we sort of supply the scientists for that
> – when you've got all the scientific work written up
> – we all sort of check it through
> – one reads and the others
> – you read aloud

          – and then you switch back and forward like this
          – and that doesn't bother you etc.

It is only in the first introductory statement that we encounter fairly complex noun phrases, *one of our main jobs in the Botanics* and *the flora of Turkey*. Elsewhere it is fairly rare to find an adjective modifying a noun. Occasionally you find one or two adjectives premodifying a noun in spoken language, but the sort of heavy premodified noun phrase (like that one) which constantly crops up in written language is very rare in most spoken language. Speakers prefer to add one piece of information at a time as in:

(1.3)   draw a square + a red square + red square + equal sided
                   + quite small side quite a small square + +

Noun phrases like *a small red equal-sided square* do not seem to occur in the spoken language as it is spoken by most speakers. Such a phrase is, of course, perfectly acceptable and normal in the written language. One major difference between spoken language and written language is the density of packing of information. It will be obvious from our discussion that information may be packed densely in the written language, using heavily premodified noun phrases with accompanying post-modification, heavy adverbial modification and complex subordinating syntax. It is rare to find spoken language produced like this, with this dense packing of information, except, as we have already said, in the speech of those who spend a lot of their time in the written language and are producing 'pre-rehearsed' opinions.

Thus spoken language which has much more in common with written language may be found in the speech of public speakers (e.g. politicians), lawyers, and academics. It is interesting, though, to note that many highly effective public speakers use comparatively 'simple language' (the British politicians Michael Foot and Enoch Powell spring to mind as examples) and that, in many universities, academic lectures are increasingly produced in the simpler style which is characteristic of spoken language – which packs in less dense information, and less highly structured information. There are good reasons to suppose that such language is a great deal easier to understand in the oral mode than 'written language spoken aloud'.

The language we have exemplified so far has been language produced by educated adult speakers. It is important for those who teach adolescents to realise that the language used by native-speaking adolescents is typically very different in some respects from the language used by adults. Consider some of the expressions cited by David Wilkins in his book *Notional Syllabuses* (1976) as examples of 'a wide range of utterances which are habitually associated with the seeking of permission'. We cite the shortest 'simplest' explicit set:

Can	
May	I use your telephone, (please)?
Could	
Might	

Might	I	possibly	use your telephone?
Could		perhaps	

All of these forms are perfectly appropriate adult forms. The first set is appropriate for adolescents (though we might note that most adolescents do not distinguish between *can* and *may* in a regular way, are more likely to use *can* than *may*, and are more likely to use the present tense forms *may* and *can* than the past tense forms *could* and *might*). The second set is much less characteristic of adolescent use, simply because adolescent spoken language typically produces much less *modality* than adult language. The combination of *might / could* (modal verbs, 'polite' past tense form) and the modal operators *possibly / perhaps* is not typical of adolescent speech (though it may be found in the speech of some a-typical teenagers brought up in highly 'modal' environments). Some of the longer forms suggested by Wilkins, while certainly possible written forms, would look unlikely as speech in the mouth of any but the most pedantic elderly scholar, or in a speaker who is 'taking the Mickey' by producing an elaborately over-polite form as in: 'Would you consent to me using your telephone?' Wilkins discusses the general difficulty of determining appropriate use, but not the particular difficulty with respect to adolescent speech. It does seem reasonable that young foreign speakers should not be taught to *produce* forms which young native speakers do not typically produce. Such an approach would not of course suggest that young foreign speakers should not encounter such expressions, appropriately used, in the mouths of adults who they observe talking on film, television, etc. They should be able to recognise such formally polite expressions. If teachers of younger students wish to ensure that their students are able to express themselves politely, it is probably far more important that they should learn to produce a polite *manner* of speaking, a polite voice quality, a polite smile, than that they should produce complex modalised expressions which merely sound 'odd' in the mouths of young speakers. Naturally, as students grow into adults, they can appropriately begin to use the more complex adult expressions.

If our characterisation of the formal differences between typical written language and typical spoken language is correct, several implications for teaching follow from this. First, it seems to be the case that rather limited syntax is required for adequate performance in producing the spoken language. As we have suggested, simple noun phrases and a very few subordinate declarative structures, together with an interrogative structure to ask questions with, appear to characterise typical spoken language produced by native speakers. Similarly, a great deal of the vocabulary which is produced is of a very general, non-specific sort: *chap, guy, individual, one, other*(one), *place, thing, be, have, got, do, fine, good, bad.* Where specific vocabulary is introduced it is often made to do a good deal of work. You will have observed this in extract (1.2):

> scientists – scientists – scientific writing – written up
> read – read – read – reading – read

and again in extract (1.3):

> square – square – square – square
> red – red
> sided – side
> quite small – quite a small

Speakers repeat not only words (and related forms) which they themselves have introduced, but forms which have been introduced by previous speakers. On the one hand this makes it clear that the same topic is still being talked about, on the other, it saves the speaker from constantly having to hunt up a different word, since he can use a form which has already been recently activated and is readily available. We suggest, then, that the first implication that follows from the assertion that the production of spoken language is relatively undemanding, in terms of syntax and vocabulary, is that students should be encouraged to talk from a very early stage since, from a *linguistic* point of view, the level demanded of them is much less stringent than that of written language. The problems in the spoken language are going to be much more concerned with on-line production, and with the question of how to find meaningful opportunities for individual students to practise using a rather minimal knowlege of the foreign language in a flexible and inventive manner, than with linguistic complexity. We discuss these problems in chapter 2.

The implications of what we have said about typical spoken language for listening comprehension are, in a sense, less encouraging. On the one hand spoken language tends towards less specific vocabulary and far more general use of items like *thing* and *do*. This initially sounds hopeful from the point of view of the foreign learner. On the other hand, it seems at least plausible that this less specific language is actually quite hard to understand unless the listener has access to information about context and background knowledge of a sort which conventional listening comprehension teaching tends not to supply. Listening comprehension consists of far more than understanding what words and sentences mean; it involves understanding what speakers mean. Until we can get some sort of handle on teaching what speakers mean by using language in particular types of context our progress in the field of teaching listening comprehension will necessarily be slow. We return to this question in chapter 3.

1.2 Functions of language

In most of the discussion so far we have simplistically assumed that there is, on the one hand, written language and, on the other hand, spoken language, and that spoken language differs from written language primarily in the way information is less densely packed in spoken language, which has implications both for syntactic structure and for vocabulary selection.

Clearly the picture is a great deal more complex than this. Written language has many different functions ranging through literary functions, expository functions (academic, legal, journalistic), to straight informative functions ('news', familial letters, domestic 'key under the doormat' type notes), to recording functions (Hansard recording Parliament, minutes of meetings, lecture notes, doctor recording patients' medical histories) etc. In each function, language is used for a somewhat different purpose, and hence takes on a somewhat different form. There are appropriate 'styles' for different functions, different 'registers' – different typical selection of vocabulary and type of structure, different conventions of organisation of information, etc. We shall now assert that the use of language in literary forms is a special, privileged outcrop on the fundamental functions of the written language. This is in no way to undervalue the function or place of literature in our lives, which, as people privileged to live in a culture with a rich literary history, we enthusiastically endorse. It seems to be a fact, however, that written literary forms emerge long after the arrival of the written language and its use for other, more basic purposes (cf. Goody, 1977). What are these other 'more basic' purposes? They appear to be recording facts about society, and the individual in society, which may give rise to dissension or unhappiness if individuals disagree about those facts; to record who owns what, who left who what in his will, what was agreed in the treaty at the end of a bout of hostilities, who agreed to pay who how much, who agreed that who should have which powers, etc. They appear to include messages, giving information about who is going where to do what and when, messages which can be left to yield up their information at a later time than the time of writing, and in a place where the writer no longer is. If we generalise across the uses of written language in our society (still excepting literature) we find that the fundamental function common to most uses of the written language is the transmission of information, whether recording information about what is past, or recording the intentions of writers about what is to happen in the future. We shall call this information-transferring function of language the *transactional* function of language. We shall assume that when the transactional function is at issue, it matters that information is clearly conveyed, since the purpose of the producer of the message is to convey information. In written language, generally, we shall expect to find the transactional function uppermost. There are genres (other than literary genres of written language) where this function is not primary: 'thank you' letters, love-letters, party games, come to mind as examples.

These last examples in many ways have in common what is clearly the overriding function of spoken language: the maintenance of social relationships. Most people spend a great deal of their everyday lives in 'chat', where the primary purpose is to be nice to the person they are talking to. Sometimes transactional spoken language is embedded within such chat. Thus a visit to the dentist or the driving instructor or the caretaker usually begins with a greeting which is followed by comments on the weather or what is happening in the world. The transactional element is then performed, and the meeting finishes up with farewells. Many social interactions seem to contain very little transactional content. People meeting on the bus or train for the first time, people meeting at parties, people meeting at the beginning of a new lecture course, will tend to conduct a type of talk where one person offers a topic for comment by the other person, responds to the other person if his topic is successful and, if it is not, proffers another topic of conversation. Such primarily interactional chats are frequently characterised by constantly shifting topics and a great deal of agreement on them. In the following extract, notice how often the speakers begin their turns with *yes* and how the conversation, even in this short extract, shifts from 'the couple' (*they*), to *sunsets*, to a *postcard*, to *last year's calendar*, to *this year's*, to *the Anderson's house*, to *the Andersons*.

(1.4)   (The preceding discussion has included a mention of a couple who visit the area each summer.)
A: you know but erm + they used to go out in erm August

+ they used to come + you know the lovely sunsets
you get + at that time and
B: oh yes
C: there's a nice new postcard a nice – well I don't know
how new it is + it's been a while since I've been here +
of a sunset + a new one +
A: oh that's a lovely one isn't it
D: yes yes it was in one of the + calendars
A: yes that was last year's calendar it was on
D: was it last year's it was on + it was John Forgan who
took that one
A: yes it's really lovely + this year's erm + the Anderson's
house at Lenimore's in it + at em Thunderguy I should
say +
D: they've sold their house
A: yes + the Andersons
B: oh have they
A: yes yes + erm + they weren't down last year at all +

It is a characteristic of speech of this kind that it should yield a
situation in which the participating speakers should end up feeling
comfortable with each other and friendly. It is very noticeable that
speakers in such 'chat' do not typically challenge each other, do not
argue, do not require repetition of something that the other person
has said. If a participant in such an interaction does not hear exactly
what it was the speaker said, he is quite likely simply to nod and
smile. The remarks we made about 'generalised' vocabulary and
sparse information-packing apply most of all to casual interactional
chat. A close post-hoc analysis of what was said in such a chat often
reveals quite large areas of unclarity and non-specificity where it
seems likely that the listener was only partially processing the
message coming in, doing the listening equivalent of 'skimming' in
reading, which we could characterise as listening for the 'gist', the
overall impression, rather than for the detail.

We assume that normal individuals in any culture easily acquire
the ability to participate in primarily interactional chat. From a very
early stage the human infant is talked to by its mother. Long before
the infant can possibly understand the language being addressed to it,
the mother addresses *yes* / *no* questions to it (particularly questions
which can be answered by *yes*), and watches the baby's face for any
flicker of muscle, produced for whatever physiological reasons,
which she can interpret as the baby agreeing with her. The infant has
long training in participating in an interaction under conditions
where it cannot be expected to understand the *language* addressed
to it. What is required is agreement and, when the infant agrees,
the mother is pleased. When toddlers are taken to visit their

grandparents, they are frequently addressed in terms which they cannot understand, even if they recognise the words, and they continue to learn that what is required is agreement. Most inter-actional chat contains, apart from more-or-less formal patterns of greeting and farewell, a great deal of expression of opinion by one participant which is then agreed to by the other, who may then take his turn in expressing opinion or merely continue to take the role of agreeing with the other, dominant, participant.

Spoken language may also have a primarily transactional function (though few speakers produce language which is not to some extent 'recipient-designed', that is carefully produced so that the listener can understand it, taking account of the listener's state of knowledge). When spoken language is used for a primarily transactional function, what is primarily at issue, as in the case of transactional written language, is the transference of information. The purpose of the speaker in speaking is primarily to communicate his message rather than to be nice to the listener. We could say that primarily interactional language is primarily *listener-oriented*, whereas primarily transactional language is primarily *message-oriented*. Primarily transactional spoken language is frequently concerned to get things done in the real world – so a boss dictates a letter, a car-salesman explains how the electric window-winding device works, a customer complains to the garage, a patient discusses her symptoms with a doctor, a teacher explains an English construction to a class, a pupil requests permission to leave the room, a hairdresser orders shampoo from a sales representative, a neighbour gives instructions about feeding his canaries while he's on holiday, a magistrate explains to a social worker the conditions of supervision for a truanting pupil, a child tells Santa Claus what she would like for Christmas. In each case the speaker is concerned to make his message clear – it matters that the listener gets it right and the speaker may well be angry, distressed, or disappointed if the listener hasn't understood correctly. If the listener doesn't understand and shows that he doesn't understand, the speaker will repeat what he has said. In some cases he will conventionally repeat it anyway. In some cases the recipient is conventionally expected to make notes in writing, in order to form a permanent record of what was said (secretary, doctor, student – each makes a record of what was said).

Speakers typically go to considerable trouble to make what they are saying clear when a transaction is involved, and may contradict the listener if he appears to have misunderstood. When the *message* is the reason for speaking, then the message must be understood. Successful transactional speech often involves more use of specific vocabulary. A driver may tell a friend that the car is behaving in a 'woozy' manner, which may be perfectly acceptable as chat between friends, but this will not be particularly helpful as an instruction to the garage mechanic. The garage mechanic will require some properties to be specified of 'woozy' like 'it makes a grating noise each time I change gear'.

In transactional situations, where information transference is the primary reason for the speaker choosing to speak, the language tends to be clearer, more specific, than in primarily interactional situations. We assume that normal speakers of a language achieve an ability to express their needs, to communicate information, at least in short bursts. Even infants only just learning to speak, typically use a good deal of that speech to acquire what they want with cries of 'more', 'icecream', 'no socks', etc. and to inform their listeners what it is they want them to pay attention to, as in exclamations of 'doggy', 'Daddy', 'car', etc. We assume that few normal speakers have much difficulty with communicating their simple transactional intentions, at least when they only need to express what they want to say rather briefly. Depending upon the complexity of the information to be communicated, however, even adult native speakers sometimes find it difficult to make clear what they want to say. We shall return to this point in the next section.

It is obvious that all foreign learners of English, who wish to learn the spoken form of the language, need to be able to express their transactional intentions. When they use language transactionally, it is important that they are able to make clear what it is they want to say. It is inappropriate to produce, or to try to interpret, in terms of this level of clarity when the purpose of speech is primarily interactional. Consider the following interaction:

(1.5)
G: I watched that film last night + remember that − did you see it
H: no I'm afraid I didn't − haven't got a television + what was −
G: it's eh + it was about eh + the assassination of + President Carter + I think it was
H: mm
G: aye it was him and you saw it it was a good film + I watched it all +
H: what happened in it
G: well eh you just saw the ashassina + assassination and there was somebody taking the part of what the man had done that got shot him eh + that shot him and they was following all the things and all that and then + eh this other man went and shot him because he liked the President + and then after that it just ended up that he got took to prison +

H: oh I see
G: so it was good + +

G is a sixteen-year-old Scottish school girl (with some dialectal, non-standard features in her speech) who is chatting, in familiar surroundings in her own school, to an interviewer. The formal part of the interview has not yet begun. G chats on and on, interactionally very competently. She checks on her listener's state of knowledge in her first utterance. When she finds that her listener did not see the film which she wants to comment on, she tells her what happened in it. Summarising and narrating the content of a film is a cognitively very difficult task. If there were some overriding transactional requirement here, the speaker would need to express what she is saying a great deal more clearly, and her listener would probably keep on interrupting to check that she understood who was doing what to whom at any given point in the summary. As it is, neither speaker nor listener comments on the inappropriateness of talking about a film which recounts the assassination of 'President Carter'. Similarly the speaker – and presumably the listener as well – does not keep a very close control over the possible referents, in the speaker's last long turn, of expressions like *the man, him, they, and all that, this other man, him, he, he.* If the listener needed to, she could probably work out who was being referred to at any given time, given that she has any background knowledge of the events portrayed in the film. It is important to realise that this lack of specificity in primarily interactional speech generally does not matter. Neither speaker nor listener needs to keep tight track of the detail.

The position with respect to primarily transactional speech is different. Here, we repeat, it really matters that what is said is clear. Consider the case where a patient goes to see a doctor. What is important for the patient is that the doctor should reassure her and make her feel better. What is important for the doctor is that he should understand what it is that the patient is complaining of. This is not simply interactional chat, this will have an effect on events in the world. Consider the following transcript of part of what a patient says to a doctor in answer to his question 'what can I do for you?':

(1.6)   Patient: well, uh, I was concerned about, uh . . . last
         summer I guess. . . I was very low in hormones,
         and he – uh – the estrogen
    Doctor: mh
    Patient: the count was so low he said I didn't get it so he
         put me on uh . . . on the estrogen pills. Now
         about four years ago when I went through Phipps,
         uh, they had cut me down to a half and I still was

getting a lot of uh swel-swelling and soreness in
my breasts and they told me to get one about
every six months, but, I sort of took myself off the
estrogen and found that I didn't have any of that
feeling . . .

(Quoted from Cicourel, 1981)

Cicourel comments that the doctor's notes of what the patient is
suffering from record different details from those which the patient
appears to have said. It is clear that speaking in this kind of interactional mode is not helpful to the cause of the transference of
information. We said above that we assume that native speakers will
generally be able to express transactional intentions 'at least when
they only need to express what they want to say rather briefly'.
How are we to account for this native speaker's apparent inability
to explain clearly what she is worried about to the doctor? We
approach this problem in the next section.

1.3 Structured long turns

In this section we are going to make a distinction between 'short
turns' and 'long turns'. A short turn consists of only one or two
utterances, a long turn consists of a string of utterances which may
last as long as an hour's lecture. There is clearly no principled point
of cut-off between them. We may note, however, that short turns do
not demand much of the speaker in the way of producing structure.
Consider the following conversation:

(1.7)
C: whisky sour mix + did you +
J: whisky sour + daiquiri +
C: do you like –
K: it was all right
C: my mother's favourite is daiquiri + but I love whisky
   sour + it's a super –
K: and marguerita I love as well – it's beautiful
C: what's that
K: it's some + it's er tequila and lime + with something
   else +
C: I don't know it
J: salt + no
K: yes and it's got the rough really rough salt round the
   edge of the glass and you drink it through the salt +
   and it's whipped up somehow
C: I've never tasted it
K: it's a Mexican drink + absolutely beautiful + really
   liked it

This primarily interactional conversation between three female, graduate, native speakers consists of swapping short turns. Even the longest of these short turns only consists of statements of additional information: *it's got the rough . . . salt, and you drink it through the salt, and it's whipped up somehow.* If you compare what is needed to contribute a short turn like this to a conversation as opposed to what is needed to summarise the content of a film (as in extract (1.5)) or to summarise your relevant medical history for your doctor (as in extract (1.6)), it immediately becomes obvious that what is required of a speaker in a long turn is considerably more demanding than what is required of a speaker in a short turn. As soon as a speaker 'takes the floor' for a long turn, tells an anecdote, tells a joke, explains how something works, justifies a position, describes an individual, and so on, he takes responsibility for creating a structured sequence of utterances which must help the listener to create a *coherent* mental representation of what he is trying to say. What the speaker says must be coherently structured. He must make it clear who or what he is talking about, and specify any relevant properties, before he moves on to saying what happened. If he is recounting a narrative, he will, conventionally, establish where and when the events happened, and who the main participant was, before he recounts the series of events. He will recount the series of events in the order in which they happened or, if for some reason he chooses not to do this, he must explicitly mark the deviation from this normal unmarked ordering. Consider the following extract:

(1.8)   there were + some very very good houses rather old-fashioned but quite good houses + with very big rooms and that + and these were sort of better class people + people with maybe + minor civil servants and things like that you know that had been able to afford + dearer rents and that in those days you know + + but the average working-class man + the wages were very small + the rents would run from anything from about five shillings to + seven shillings which was about all they could've possibly afforded in those days . . .

This is a long turn taken by an elderly man reminiscing about how things were when he was young. He has mentioned a particular area of the town. He goes on to say that there were, in that part of the town, *very very good houses*; he then adds some properties to those houses: *rather old-fashioned, quite good houses, with very big rooms.* He then speaks of the people who lived in those houses, *minor civil servants,* and the essential requisite shared by such people *that had been able to afford + dearer rents.* He then contrasts the condition of people who could afford to live in such houses with the condition of *the average working-class man* who only earned *very small wages*, only enough to pay a very small rent *from about five shillings to + seven shillings*. The structure of progression in this extract is reasonably easy to perceive. It is by no means always made explicit by the speaker, and the listener has to do a certain amount of work to see how the succeeding statements fit together to form a coherent representation of what the population in that part of the town was like and why. Consider now a further long turn by another elderly speaker reminiscing about his past:

(1.9) I was + I was only eh + I was seven when the First World War broke out + I can remember the First World War though + I can remember + soldiers marching up the Canongate you know + of course being a kid and + following the band and + you know thinking it was wonderful and I can remember soldiers coming home + with mud still on them and all that sort of thing + these are things that do stick in your memory

This speaker begins by relating himself at the tender age of seven to the breaking out of *the First World War* and follows this by stating that, despite this early age, he can *remember the First World War*. He then gives examples of some memories, *soldiers marching up the Canongate*; and remarks that *being a kid* (of seven or so), *following the band* (presumably the band leading the marching soldiers), he thought it *was wonderful*. He then adds a further, different memory, presumably of later in the War, *soldiers coming home*; and then generalises, *these are things that do stick in your memory*. Just as the previous speaker moved from a part of town to houses in that part of town, to people living in those houses, gradually narrowing down, so this speaker begins with a global statement about remembering *the First World War* and then narrows down to *the soldiers marching* and *the band*. In each case it is not difficult to perceive a structure in what the speaker says.

The third example of a long turn is provided by a young woman who is commenting on recent changes in a part of Edinburgh:

(1.10) actually I was coming down the Grassmarket + today and + it's quite nice just now the Grassmarket since + it's always had the antique shops but they're looking − they're em become a bit nicer and they've got the fair down there too which is + the Grassmarket Fair on the left hand side + it's an open-air market + er not an open-air market it's an indoor market on the left-hand side you know

She first identifies what she's talking about, *the Grassmarket*; and gives her credentials for having an opinion about it, *I was coming down . . . today*; and provides some properties for it, *it's quite nice just now* (general), *it's always had the antique shops* (particular); and adds some properties to them, *but they're looking . . . become a bit nicer.* She then adds a further piece of information about the Grassmarket, *they've got the fair down there too*; and further specifies 'the fair', *the Grassmarket Fair on the left-hand side*; adds a further piece of information about 'the fair', *it's an open-air market*; realises she has said the wrong thing, and corrects herself. Again, even in this rather loose interactional description, it is possible to discern a structure, a structure of the kind which necessarily underlies long turns which clearly do not consist simply of lists of unstructured statements.

The ability to construct such long turns appears to vary with individuals, in part, no doubt, depending on the opportunity they have had to produce long turns which other people bother to listen to. The ability to produce long transactional turns, in which clear information is transferred, is, we claim, not an ability which is automatically acquired by all native speakers of a language. It is an ability which appears to need adequate models, adequate practice and feedback. Several recent surveys in Britain have thrown up comments by employers, potential employers, Income Tax offices, Social Security offices and other public services, that many school-leavers, particularly among those who leave school at sixteen, are 'inarticulate'. We assume that this means that they do not succeed in transferring information effectively in long turns. The patient describing her medical history (extract (1.6)), and many of the extracts we cite in chapter 4, exemplify partial failure to com-municate information in transactional long turns.

How does this finding affect foreign language teaching? If such a large number of native English speakers find difficulty with communicating information effectively in long turns, it seems reasonable to suppose that native speakers of other languages may suffer from the same disadvantage. If one of the demands in the English syllabus turns out to be transferring information effectively in English, it may be that the most satisfactory response to the problem would be first to train the student to talk effectively in this mode in the native language before being required to perform this cognitively complex task in the foreign language.

The general point which needs to be made, however, is that it is important that the teacher should realise that simply training the student to produce short turns will not automatically yield a student who can perform satisfactorily in long turns. It is currently fashionable in language teaching to pay particular attention to the forms and function of short turns – regarded in a 'communicative' or 'functional' light, in terms of categories of 'speech acts'. This seems an excellent development in the early stages of language learning, in that it is a development which appears to mirror the normal acquisition of language skills in all cultures. It must be clear, however, that exclusive concentration on short turns throughout the curriculum will yield speakers who are only able to take part in the sort of conversation we illustrated in extract (1.7). Indeed if the behests of some courses which deal exclusively with 'speech acts' uttered in complete sentences are taken seriously, the foreign speaker will not actually be able to participate in a conversation of that sort, but only perform in highly dramatic conversations caricatured in the following extract:

(1.11)   A: (greets B) Good morning.
                B: (greets A) Good morning.
                A: (requests) Might I possibly borrow your garden fork?
                B: (agrees) Yes. (warns) It's rather heavy.
                A: (accepts) Oh. (thanks) Thank you very much. (apologises) I'm sorry I stuck it in your foot.
                B: (accepts apology) That's all right. (generalises) I'm used to it. (warns) Careful you don't do it. (exclaims) You have! (offers) Can I lend you some iodine?
                A: (accepts) Yes, please. (thanks) Thank you.

The concern with teaching short turns arises fairly naturally from the traditional view in language teaching, which was that the only structure the student was required to master was the sentence. Recently the focus of attention has shifted from the form of the sentence to the functions it can be used to perform. This should yield a student who is able to produce correct sentences in a short turn, responding correctly to an identified social stimulus. It must surely be clear that students who are only capable of producing short turns are going to experience a lot of frustration when they try to speak the foreign language. They may have achieved basic interactional skills and they may have the language forms available to permit them to request information, services etc., but they are very far indeed from the expressed aim of many courses which is to permit the students to 'express themselves' in the foreign language. In chapters 2 and 4 we return to this problem.

1.4 Spoken language models and feasibility

One of the pleasures of teaching the written language is that it is so easy to provide good models of almost any kind of writing. Models of texts created for different purposes can be provided and models of sentences created for different purposes. And in each case the model is one which the student can profitably base his own production on. If he copies the model carefully, the teacher can tell him that what he produces is 'right'.

This comfortable notion of 'correctness' is a good deal less obvious when it comes to teaching the spoken language. It is not at all obvious what sort of model is appropriate to offer the foreign learner since native spoken language so obviously reflects the 'performance' end of the *competence–performance* distinction. It reveals so many examples of slips, errors, incompleteness, produced by the speaker, speaking in the *here-and-now*, under pressure of time, trying to tie in what he is saying *now* with what he has just said, and while he is simultaneously working out what he is about to say. Clearly the foreign student should not be *taught* to produce incomplete sentences. The teacher has to work out some satisfactory compromise. Presumably, in the early stages, students will be offered, as models to copy directly, short complete sentences and phrases produced by the teacher. When the student attempts to reproduce such model phrases and sentences in 'conversation' exercises, it seems reasonable that he should not be corrected if he produces partial sentences, incomplete phrases, of the sort produced by native speakers. When the student listens to native speakers talking, most of the time listening to language produced spontaneously, he should realise that speakers of this foreign language talk like human beings, like he talks in his native language. They don't produce ideal strings of complete, perfectly formed, sentences. They use language manipulatively, exploratorily, to communicate with and make up what they say as they go along.

It is sometimes said of some foreign speakers of English, particularly speakers from northern Europe, that they speak language which is 'more perfect' than that spoken by native English speakers, because they produce complete sentences and articulate clearly. A recent article in *The Guardian* newspaper said just this of some Russian speakers of English. The only way you could tell they were foreign, it said, was because they spoke English so 'perfectly'. This is a very odd notion of 'perfection'. The effect, as a native speaker being addressed by a foreign speaker with such 'perfect English', is that one is being addressed as if one were an audience at a public meeting, where the speaker is speaking formally and precisely on a matter which he has thought about many times before. The language may be *formally* correct but it is certainly *inappropriate*, and the reaction of many native speakers of English might reasonably be that it is quite hard to feel friendly towards someone who

addresses you as if you were an audience at a public meeting. It
would seem more sensible in a syllabus for advanced learners to
concentrate on exposing them to a range of modes of speech
appropriate to different contexts of situation, than to demand of
them an unreasonable 'non-native' standard of 'correctness' in all
situations.

A necessary corollary of an educational system which puts great
emphasis on 'correctness' in speaking a foreign language must be that
many students feel themselves to be failures, since only relatively
few, exceptional, individuals will achieve this ability to hold
conversations in which they produce exclusively 'correct' and
'complete' forms.

It is worthwhile considering what the motivation for students
learning a foreign language is, in determining the content of their
curricula. Most students, it seems, would like to be able to speak the
foreign language very well, but retain their cultural identity. This is
interpretable as meaning that they would like to understand fairly
easily what is said to them. It follows that they will require a lot of
training in listening comprehension. In spoken production it means
that they should control a range of abilities from taking short turns in
primarily interactive 'chat' to taking longer transactional turns. As
you will see from the transcripts of native speakers talking which we
pepper this book with, native speakers relatively rarely produce
complete correct sentences in spoken language. It seems reasonable
then that foreign students should not be obliged to do so all of the
time, since to do so merely makes them sound very foreign. In spoken
production it probably means that students are not going to be highly
motivated to improve their pronunciation beyond a certain point.
Most students identify 'how they speak' with their own personal and
cultural identities. Many foreign speakers of English who have lived
in Britain for twenty or thirty years understand English just about
perfectly, and produce English just about perfectly in every respect,
except that they still retain a foreign accent. Many such French,
Polish, Hungarian, or Gujerati speakers wish to produce the
language like native speakers in every respect save that of pronunciation. They wish to preserve their own identities to be known
to be, say, a French speaker speaking superb English, not to be
taken for an Englishman or a Welshman. Of course there are a few
rare individuals who are superb mimics and quickly adopt a native-
like pronunciation, often in a variety of languages – splendid
potential undercover agents. Such individuals appear to be able to do
this quite independently of the educational system. It would be
absurd to suppose that a performance of this kind should be the
target set by an educational system since it would necessarily follow

that the vast majority of both teachers and students would spend most of their time feeling that they were failures. A more reasonable approach would seem to be one where a much more relaxed attitude to 'correctness' is adopted, and many more students can attain success.

1.5 Feasibility – what can be taught?

We have said that the primary function of written language is *transactional*, to convey information (though there are relatively major exceptions, like literature, and relatively minor interactional ones like love letters). We have said that the primary function of spoken language is *interactional*, to establish and maintain social relations. However, an important function of spoken language is primarily transactional – to convey information. We shall schematically represent these functions in figure 1.1.

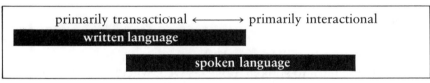

Figure 1.1   *Functions of language*

Notice that spoken language, while mostly under 'primarily interactional', protrudes well under 'primarily transactional' as well (where it will often be associated, as we pointed out, with note-taking, i.e with the written language).

In language teaching it seems reasonable to assume that much of what the student has learnt about the nature of primarily interactional speech in his own language can be transferred to the foreign language. It may be necessary to bring to his attention what happens in his native language, since our 'knowledge' of such communicative matters is usually held well below the level of consciousness. Listening analytically to a tape of what goes on in the student's native language may be a valuable preamble to listening to a similar tape in the target language. Much of what the student produces in primarily interactional language may be modelled more or less directly on his native language experience, and on the tapes which he hears in listening comprehension classes.

In primarily transactional spoken language the problem is different. As we have demonstrated (and will further demonstrate in detail in chapter 4) many native speakers of a language have particular difficulty with controlling extended transactional turns. The performance of native speakers can be improved by training. It seems reasonable to suggest that the explicit teaching of the production of the spoken form of the foreign language should be particularly concerned with the teaching of extended transactional turns. For one reason, because these are likely to prove difficult for most speakers; for another, because foreign students visiting a native-speaking English country will have to cope in an indus-trialised, bureaucratised, society which depends very much on the ability of individuals to use spoken language to communicate information efficiently; for yet another reason, because foreign students who require spoken English out of a native-speaking context are likely to require it primarily for transactional reasons, for acquiring and disseminating information; and, lastly, as we shall suggest in chapter 2, it is methodologically much more feasible to teach control of transactional turns than to teach explicit control of interactional turns.

1.6 Texts

The word 'text' is familiar as applied to the written language. We shall apply the term to spoken 'texts' as well, where 'text' means 'verbal record of communication'. We shall assume that the taped record we deal with has 'primary' status, and that the transcript we accompany it with represents our *interpretation* of what was said. In some cases the tape may not be clear and your interpretation may differ from ours. The same is almost certainly true of a great deal that we listen to in our everyday lives. We all construct reasonable interpretations which we assume do, for the most part, coincide. It would be a mistake, in teaching the spoken language, to assume that it is always clear what the speaker said, or what he intended to say (even to him), or to suppose that there is only one single 'correct' interpretation of the smudged acoustic signal which the speaker produces. Throughout this book we shall constantly appeal to the notion of 'reasonable interpretation of a text' rather than 'correct interpretation of a text'.

2 Teaching spoken production

2.0 The production of spoken language

Spoken language production, learning to talk in the foreign language, is often considered to be one of the most difficult aspects of language learning for the teacher to help the student with. The practical problems are obvious. In written production, each writer can get on by himself, without disturbing the rest of the class, at his own speed. In comprehension classes, whether written or spoken, the whole class can receive the same stimulus at the same time and each student can do whatever task is required of him by himself. In the production of speech, however, each speaker needs to speak. He needs to speak individually and, ideally, he needs someone to listen to him speaking and to respond to him. When he speaks, he makes a noise which will disturb other students unless they are saying the same thing at the same time, or unless they are listening to what he says. The possible ways of coping with this seem to be limited. You find choral practice of language which is written down, or learned, or which copies an immediately preceding model. You find students giving individual short responses to the teacher's questions. You find students working with language lab courses without disturbing anyone else, which may give a simulated feeling that there is a listener present and where, from time to time, the teacher may overhear what the student is saying and correct it. In rare, privileged, environments, you occasionally find small-group 'conversation' classes where eight to ten people talk together in the foreign language.

In courses which are conducted on the basis of large-group teaching or language lab practice, there must necessarily be a premium on 'correctness' in spoken language production. The student is frequently expected to 'reply in complete sentences' when the teacher asks him a question in class, since, if he simply says *yes* or *no*, he gets so little practice in producing the spoken form. The language he produces is, typically, evaluated by the teacher for its correctness, either with respect to pronunciation or to grammar or both. In the language lab, the pre-ordained correct response frequently takes the form of a short, complete, sentence. Again, if this

Teaching spoken production

is evaluated at all, it is likely to be evaluated in terms of correctness of pronunciation or grammar.

In chapter 1 we discussed the problem of 'the model' for spoken English production and raised the question of the appropriateness of a sentence-based model in descriptions of spoken language. Perhaps the most widespread assumption in teaching the spoken language is that the sentence is the appropriate unit of planning and performance. Yet native speakers typically produce bursts of speech which are much more readily relateable to the phrase – typically shorter than sentences, and only loosely strung together. If native speakers typically produce short, phrase-sized chunks, it seems perverse to demand that foreign learners should be expected to produce complete sentences. Indeed it may demand of them, in the foreign language, a capacity for forward-planning and storage which they rarely manifest in speaking their own native language. 'Correctness', in terms of complete sentences, seems an inappropriate notion in spoken language.

'Correctness' in terms of pronunciation is also, as we have remarked, a frequent goal in spoken language programmes. The norm for those learning to speak British English is usually taken to be 'RP' – that southern British, non-rhotic accent, which is also called 'Oxford English' or 'BBC English'. After years of rigorous attention to pronunciation during the fifties and early sixties, many teachers now accept that the aim of achieving native-like pronunciation is not only unattainable but unreasonable, for the reasons we discussed in section 1.4. Nowadays the teacher probably tries to achieve the set of phonological contrasts which is manifested in RP, but does not worry too much about the phonetic detail. He ignores delicacies like whereabouts an 'r' is produced, and whether an 'l' is light or dark, and is simply grateful if the student can produce an opposition between 'l' and 'r'. After all there are native accents of British English which manifest uvular 'r' and 'light' 'l's. The only students who need to have highly polished accents are those who are going to be English teachers. Most of these accept that they are not about to go into the business of working as undercover agents, but are simply Italian or Danish or Egyptian teachers speaking English (very well) with an Italian or Danish or Egyptian accent. It is rarely demanded, nowadays, of native English teachers that they should lose their Yorkshire or Somerset accents. It is only required of such teachers that what they say should produce clear and not 'heavily accented' English. They do not seek to become RP speakers. Neither need foreign learners. There do still exist spoken production courses for foreign students which appear to wish to exact a native-like standard of RP pronunciation. Less competent students in particular are likely to find courses which place a strong emphasis on pronunciation extremely boring, an attitude which leads to them becoming increasingly less competent. That minority of competent students who emerge from a course with good pronunciation seem to gain more spontaneously mimicking good models than from hours spent drilling vowels and consonants and words in isolation.

Used well, language learning experience based on notions of 'correct responses' may enable the student to improve his pronunciation and to improve his ability to produce short structured responses in familiar dialogue slots. What it obviously cannot prepare him to do is produce an extended response, to take a 'long turn', since it gives him no practice in producing extended responses. Neither does it prepare the student to make the spoken foreign language 'work' for him, by working out what he wants to say by saying it and then modifying it, which is how many of us use spoken language much of the time. Curiously, the assessment which follows a course composed of short, structured 'correct' responses, often demands that the student should produce an extended stretch of speech in a 'prepared talk' on some topic – a type of activity which the course has in no way prepared him for.

2.1 The aims of the course

What should a course in spoken English production prepare a student to do? The intention is, often, that the student should be able to 'express himself' in the target language, to cope with basic interactive skills like exchanging greetings and thanks and apologies, and to express his 'needs' – request information, services etc. Note that that simple assertion implies two quite different sorts of course, or at least two quite different components of a course. The syllabus which results from a 'needs' or 'notions' approach will prepare a student to produce short turns of a transactional and/or interactional type. It will be largely unstructured, because there is no obvious way in which the ability to express an apology builds upon the ability to express thanks, or in which the ability to express a request builds upon the ability to express a warning. Such a syllabus will consist, essentially, of a list of forms which may be used to perform a range of social/cognitive functions. The forms will tend to be 'sentence types' and the functions will tend to be identified as 'act types', speech acts which are performed by uttering a short sentence, taking a short turn. However, the syllabus which results from taking seriously an expression like 'enabling the speaker to express himself' must surely go beyond short turns and consider what it would mean for a speaker to be responsible for the structure of a long turn and to consider, further, whether some types of long turn are 'easier' in some sense than others. It should consider whether there are strategies for controlling long turns which a speaker can usefully be taught. If there are 'easier' types of long turn, and if there are helpful strategies, then a teacher might be able to construct a structured course where a student could learn a simple skill before building on that to achieve a more complex skill. In such a course, it would be clear that a student could 'make progress' rather than simply 'learn another set of things to say'. The teacher would be in the position of controlling a set of strategies which would help the student 'improve' his performance. If a student had difficulty in 'expressing himself' in conversation classes, the teacher might be able to diagnose his problem and give him practice in helpful strategies, rather than simply attributing the student's problems to his inability to 'learn' what his peers have learnt. The teacher needs to be in the confident position of possessing analytic tools which enable him to determine where the difficulty lies and to help the student with it. We are far from being in the position of being able to provide a readymade pack of such analytic strategies for all occasions, but in section 2.3 we propose the beginnings of a limited approach, which might permit the teacher to support and develop the student's ability to use language communicatively over a range of situations. We shall be concerned not so much with the process by which the student comes to learn the forms of the language, since many years of language teaching have been devoted to that discussion, but with the process by which the student may come to use those forms creatively and appropriately.

2.2 Interactional short turns

There is a difficulty in perceiving a principled order in which to introduce interactional short turns but, in many ways, it seems natural to teach the beginning learner appropriate language for participating in simple conversations. It is possible to perceive some, somewhat shadowy, principles of ordering. One might, for instance, suggest that there is less 'communicative stress' on a beginning student if he takes the part in a conversation of the person who responds to what somebody else says, who reacts to someone else's topic and can, therefore, use the first speaker's language to build his own response on. This is of course the basis for many audio-visual materials and of the large-class, teacher-dominated method where the materials, or the teacher, constantly take the initiative and the student is simply required to respond. A course in interactional short turns might begin with 'short responses', continue with ways of expanding what the previous speaker has said and, finally, suggest forms which would enable the speaker to take the initiative and introduce a topic of his own. Here we shall only consider some of the forms required for making the minimal 'short responses'. We shall go on to illustrate the use of such short responses in extracts from conversations.

1 The speaker agrees to co-operate or not (as in answering 'Can you help me?):
   yes, of course
   right
   right, I will
   sure, of course
   sorry, I can't
   I really can't manage it
   I'm afraid not

2 The speaker agrees with what has been said. In English, as in many other languages, it is not conversationally usual to produce a simple *yes* or *no* response. In friendly conversations the speaker normally produces at least a 'doublet':
   yes, it is
   yes, that's right
   of course it is
   quite, absolutely true
   yes, I do / yes, he was / yes, they were, etc.

3 The speaker politely disagrees. Since the purpose of interactional conversation is to produce agreement, disagreement tends to be expressed in a roundabout way:
   well not really
   not quite, no
   perhaps not quite as bad / good / difficult, as that
   erm, I don't know

4 The speaker may merely indicate 'possible doubt' as in:
   I'm not quite sure
   really?
   is that right?
   is that so?
   are you sure?

5 The speaker needs to be able to express an opinion. He needs a set of 'good' expressions and a set of 'bad' expressions and a set of modifiers to attach to these:
   very nice indeed (good, clear, pretty etc.)
   really nice
   quite nice

not very nice
not at all (etc.)
very nasty indeed (disagreeable, bad, noisy, difficult etc.)
really nasty (etc.)

Where the complementary relation exists in the mother-tongue between the understated *not nice at all* and the forthrightly asserted *very nasty indeed*, the refinement of using such comments appropriately may be attractive to the learner. It is part of the relevant 'background knowledge' of English to know that southern English speakers, in particular, have a preference for using the understated forms in some situations, and to know which situations those are.

6 The speaker needs a set of 'fillers' which will let him make it clear that he has taken up his turn or intends to continue with his turn, but is planning what to say. The most frequent native English initial responses to a direct question are *well, erm, er* (in any order) interspersed with pauses. Other 'filling' noises include *ah, uhm, mhm*.

There is a wide range of phrases which are used by native speakers to preface and interject into remarks which, being 'prefabricated', permit the speaker planning time, for instance the speaker may express his commitment to belief in what he is saying by *of course, obviously, it's clear that* as opposed to *perhaps, I think, I suppose*.

7 He needs a set of highly general vocabulary items which he can use in a flexible way to construct 'short responses', words like:
do, be, come, get, can, know
thing, bit, person, one, side, place
bit, little, nice, small, good, easy, hard, etc.

8 He needs a few simple structures:
(I think) it's a good one / it's good / it's really / very nice
(of course) he's difficult / it's no good etc.

Armed with a fairly minimal productive arsenal like this, the learner can participate in a conversation with a speaker who is prepared to do most of the work. Consider the contributions made by each of the second speakers in the extracts from native speaker conversations which follow:

(2.1)   A: you will have seen a lot of changes if you've lived in Edinburgh
    B: well + yes + ah ha + really + most of them not very nice actually + + a few quite nice ones

(2.2)   A: there was no ele + there was no electricity and there were trees and everything all over the road + it was quite frightening
    B: terrible

(2.3)   A: the next day they go round to people's houses
           B: hm hmm
           A: but + eh + it was very good
           B: ah ha
           A: and very friendly + and nobody got too obstreperous
              as they do here
           B: (laughs)
           A: but I – I thoroughly enjoyed myself
           B: good + great

(2.4)   A: she goes up north and takes eh + recordings of singing
           B: oh + + yes + that's lovely

(2.5)   A: you buy a ticket for a week or two weeks and you can
              travel wherever you like + my grandson bought one
              for a month
           B: uhuh
           A: an Ameripass you call it
           B: that's right + that's right
           A: this time last year he was there + three and a half
              months
           B: ah + great

(2.6)   A: you meet people in funny ways
           B: amazing + yes +

(2.7)   A: did you like it
           B: great + fine + fantastic

(2.8)   A: were you watching TV last night + I put up with it + I
              wouldn't say I watched it + did you watch it on
              Saturday
           B: I watched it on Saturday
           A: did you see the supporters + their own supporters +
              were booing them
           B: yes + they were booing them

In these snippets from primarily interactive conversations the
individual B is, in each case, responding to A who 'has the floor'. The
typical response is, as we see, to react to what A has said (e.g. by
laughing), to comment on what A has said (*good*, *great*, etc.) or to
reply to questions. Note particularly speaker B's strategy in (2.8)
where she picks up the phrases used by A and incorporates them into
her reply. It is clear that the role of B in each case can be taken by
someone who has at least some idea of what the incoming message
means, together with a rather limited control of output.

Obviously B's role rapidly becomes immensely frustrating, since he
is limited to responding and is unable to initiate and to 'express
himself'. Many of us have found that it is fairly unsatisfactory trying
to communicate in a foreign language if you are armed only with

short sentences and expressions culled from a tourist's phrase-book. Even if we accept that B has to take a rather limited role to begin with, it rapidly becomes obvious that it is very difficult to provide the supportive senior role in a one-to-one conversation in the classroom. The opportunities for practice, if the teacher is the only 'senior' conversationalist available, are obviously limited. It seems likely that any serious attempt at practising spoken English would involve mixing learners at different levels for conversation practice, so that advanced level students would take the senior role in a conversation and support the relative beginner. It is still, in principle, hard to sustain institutionalised 'chat' for timetabled periods of time. The topic of conversation may wander too wide for the junior partner to understand enough to justify the senior partner's efforts. A better answer may be to provide the structure for a transactional con-versation, which both partners may be prepared for, in ways we shall discuss later, and to suggest that they spend a minute or two at the beginning of the period in interactional chat, with the senior partner telling the junior partner, for instance, what he has been doing in the past week. Such practice is probably valuable for both participants. For the teacher, there still remains the problem of introducing an appropriate range of expressions, structures, and vocabulary to the students and giving them opportunities to observe the appropriate use of such language. Here the tape-recorder or, very much better, the video recorder comes into its own. Students are exposed to videos or tapes of naturally occurring conversations between two people within the same age range as themselves. They may fail to understand the content of a good deal of the conversation. (We shall discuss this further in chapter 3 when we focus on listening comprehension. We merely note in passing that as adult native speakers we not infrequently have only a partial understanding of some conversation we are participating in, and that children acquiring their native language are exposed to a very great deal of speech which they only partially understand.) One purpose of studying such conversations in *production* classes would be to observe the behaviour of the 'junior' partner in conversation, to observe what expressions are used, and how the speaker integrates the verbal expressions with facial expressions, gestures, etc. We are proposing that such conversations should be used as models for the learners.

The reason for insisting on 'naturally occurring' conversations as models is that scripted dialogues may sound 'naturalistic', but what they sound 'naturalistic' *as* is as scripted dialogues. That is, there are conventions for structures in scripted dialogues which native speakers are very familiar with and immediately recognise. These are, in many respects however, characteristically different from the conventions of structures in naturally occurring conversation. The plays of Harold Pinter bear very little resemblance to transcripts of naturally occurring conversation. The same is true of many well-loved films, and TV and radio series. One obvious comment to make on the difference is that, whereas many scripted conversations are interesting, most naturally occurring conversations are extremely boring unless you happen to be an active engaged participant in one. It is quite rare that it is actually interesting to overhear a conversation unless it is about oneself or gossip. Conversations are for the people who are participating in them to achieve their purposes in – being friendly, hospitable, comforting, or whatever. They usually concern local, transitory, matters and deal with purely personal concerns. The study of 'authentic' conversations which are to be used as conversational models should not, therefore, be extended for very long at a time. The attention of the students should be focused only on those elements that they are supposed to be paying attention to. They should be led to observe particularly important features, characteristic of the type of conversation being illustrated, and, as soon as possible, put these observations to use.

2.3   Transactional turns

In section 2.2 we have discussed some of the problems which confront the teacher who wants to teach his students to participate in primarily interactive conversation. Without doubt this is one of the most difficult skills to teach students in anything remotely like a naturalistic setting.

The task of teaching students to control primarily transactional language looks a good deal more reasonable. Transactional language, language used for the transferring of information, can be taught in the context of a specific transactional task. We can bring analytic techniques to bear on tasks of different types, and on different conditions under which the student may be asked to perform the task; and we can, in principle, construct a course graded in terms of difficulty. In the sections which follow, we outline some of the principles we believe can properly be applied to the development of such a course. Some of the principles which we suggest are well known in EFL, some are tried and tested in the teaching of English as a native language, and some derive from trying to take a commonsense view of the problem. None should be accepted uncritically. In every case the teacher should consider how far what is asserted here applies to his own students and to himself.

'Communicative stress'

It seems reasonable to suggest that there are conditions under which a speaker feels more comfortable in producing what he has to say, and conditions under which he feels less comfortable. We assume that the student is more likely to produce the best that he is capable of in a foreign language under conditions where he is under least 'communicative stress'. What are the conditions which relate to communicative stress? We suggest that these include the following.

1 Features of the context:
   i) the listener – it is easier for the speaker if the listener is one of his peers or 'junior' to him. It is easier for him to talk to one listener than to many.
   ii) the situation – it is easier for the speaker if he is speaking in a familiar, private environment.

2 State of knowledge of the listener:
   i) the language – it is helpful for the speaker if the listener knows as much of the target language as the speaker does.
   ii) the information – it is helpful for the speaker if he has information which the listener does not have but which the listener, for some reason, needs. This puts the speaker firmly in control of the information and motivates him to communicate that information.

3 Type of task:
   i) status of knowledge – it is helpful for the speaker if the information he has control of is of a familiar sort so that he understands it thoroughly. It is helpful if he is familiar with the foreign-language vocabulary which is essential to the completion of the task.
   ii) structure of the task – it is helpful to the speaker if the information in the task provides its own structure so that the language is externally supported by the requirements of the task. Thus it is easier for any speaker to give an account of a series of events than it is to provide an argument for *why* those events occurred in that order.

A difficult task, which would impose considerable communicative stress, would be one where a student is obliged to tell an unfamiliar external examiner, in unfamiliar surroundings, why a dog salivates when a bell rings, in circumstances where he does not fully understand the reason, does not command the necessary language, and believes the examiner knows the answer already. Naturally such an extreme task is rarely encountered. However, it is surprising how often students are required to reconstruct a story from a set of cartoons, say, which a sympathetic examiner is sitting and looking at. It may not be at all clear what the student is expected to produce, as he makes more or less sophisticated assumptions about the examiner's pretended state of ignorance. Another frequent exercise is to require a student to stand up in class and tell the class about 'what he did at the weekend'. Unless he has been provided with very clear models of what is expected from such a task, this is going to be very difficult for the student. He has to extract from his mass of experience over the weekend some chunk, which can have some structure or meaning attributed to it, and, in order to give an account of it, he has to imagine how much background knowledge of the circumstances is shared by the teacher and the other members of the class, *and* he has to find the language appropriate to express what he wants to say. Many students speaking in their own native language find this an appallingly difficult task. Here are two fairly typical responses from native adolescents, recorded in an interview, when faced with an extremely general question. The hesitations and brief replies would not be taken as evidence that the interviewees cannot use the English language, but that they are unsure about what constitutes an answer to such an open question.

(2.9)   A: what do you like doing with your free time?
         B: going to discos + + (long silence)
         A: yeah + anything else?
         B: babysitting + +

(2.10)   A: What do you like doing with your free time?
         B: em + going to judo + + em sometimes I go
             swimming + +

A relatively easy task, by these criteria, would be one where the student has to tell another student how to do something which he, the speaker, knows how to do, and which the listener does not know how to do but wants to know how to do. Practice in transferring information will be best organised if students work in pairs, where one gives another the information needed in order to complete a task. The problem is made more difficult if the speaker has to address a group of five or six other students who also have to complete the task – under these circumstances the student is more likely to experience a 'them' and 'me' reaction, especially if he is floundering somewhat in a foreign language.

In the early stages, when students have relatively little of the foreign language available to them and need all possible support systems, it is easiest if the speaker is able to point to relevant features of whatever it is the listener is completing, and is encouraged to use English deictic expressions like *this – here, that over there* or simple phrases like *this one on top, those at the bottom, the red one next* etc. Later on, when the deictic terms are well established and the students need less support, the listeners can be seated behind a low screen which shields what they are doing from the speaker's gaze. At this point the speaker has to rely on language alone to express what he means.

A simple accessible example of what we mean by 'external support' or 'structure' to a task can be provided by considering an occasion where one student shows another how to do a card-trick which the speaker knows well, but the listener does not know. Assume that they both have the necessary vocabulary for the task – i.e. names of suits, numbers up to ten, names of 'royal cards', a 'place' imperative like *put*, a series of spatial expressions like *next to, to the left / right of, on top of* and *underneath*, some temporal 'fillers' like *next* and *now*, a minimal imperative structure and some knowledge of constraints on co-occurrence of phrases containing prepositions. Now the speaker tells the listener the first thing to do and, as he says this, he suits the actions to the words by doing it. As he tells the listener the next thing to do, again he does it as he speaks. The external action supports the language. The speaker thoroughly understands what he is talking about, and is not worried by 'memory' problems, or by selecting what it is that he has to say next, since the structure of the card-trick determines what he needs to say next. He does not have to worry about how much he needs to explain to his listener in terms of background knowledge, since he knows that his listener knows about cards in general but does not know this particular trick. As far as possible, communicative stress has been kept to a minimum.

It is, in principle, possible to create a situation near the beginning of a foreign language course where communicative stress is, as far as possible, diminished, and where, during the course the communicative stress index on some of the variables we have mentioned is deliberately manipulated to give the student, when he is ready, the opportunity of practice in speaking in more stressful situations. He may eventually be required to address more people, to explain something he has not fully understood, to defend a position he does not hold, to create a structured account of an event which has no obvious structure, to give an account of an event which he knows his listeners have no previous experience of, or one where some of his listeners are extremely knowledgeable on a topic but others are quite ignorant, and so on. It is not hard to think of conditions which make a task type more difficult. It does demand some imaginative consideration to perceive the variables which the teacher has the power to manipulate, which would provide the student with the most supportive possible environment to speak in when he begins to talk in the foreign language.

An obvious problem for the teacher arises when students are set to work in pairs where one takes the senior role (communicating the information) and the other takes the junior role (completing the required task). If the two are genuinely working together and deliberately placed in a 'private' one-to-one situation, the teacher cannot overhear what the speaker is saying and has no way of 'correcting' the speaker's output or, indeed, of checking that the speaker is speaking English. The need for the students to have opportunity for practising spoken English probably overrides these objections. The first problem is probably better ignored anyway since, as we have already suggested, few things are more discouraging to the production of a foreign language than to be interrupted and corrected (or even to know that someone is hovering beside you *ready* to interrupt and correct). Practice sessions should be regarded as practice sessions rather than as direct teaching sessions. Of course some teaching can be associated with them – the teacher can provide some required vocabulary first, write it on the board for instance, and the students can monitor their own problems and ask, while they are doing the task or even afterwards, how to say what they want to say but do not know how to say. Here the teacher is in the best of all professional teaching positions – being in control of and able to supply information which a student actually needs and is asking for, *at the moment of his need*, rather than pushing down him information which he has no active current interest in. By putting the student in a position where he is required to communicate some information, for a purpose, the teacher provides him with communicative needs, as well as putting him in a position of minimal communicative stress.

Grading tasks: events in time

Most people spend a good deal of their lives holding friendly conversations with other people. In such conversations, people typically tell each other about their experiences – what happened on the way to work this morning, what happened on their holidays, or what film they saw last night. In primarily interactional con-versation, it is often not important that the listener gets the exact details of what transpired absolutely correct – he is probably only half-listening anyway, because the typical response of most people when they listen to someone else telling an anecdote is to start preparing one of their own, which is ready to tell as soon as the current speaker has stopped speaking. Extracts (2.11)–(2.14) illustrate this sequencing from a number of conversations between different speakers.

(2.11)   A: and eh + I flew from Inverness to Stornaway + it was eleven pounds single
            B: uh huh
            A: and that's a short flight + it was only twenty minutes
            B: good heavens ++ I paid twenty-one pounds from Stornaway to Glasgow + single + on a cheap day

(2.12)   A: I never give the milk boy a tip
            B: well + the milk boy with us + has got a problem just now + because it's exactly two pounds + so he can't very well get a tip out of that

(2.13)   A: I find my grandpa is really funny on the telephone 'cos if I phone him up + he never says anything + he picks up the phone + and waits to hear from you ++
            B: hmhm
            A: I say + Grandpa you're supposed to say 'hallo' + or say the number + or something (laughs) + 'cos you don't know if the line's + gone dead or what
            B: I have an aunt + I have an aunt who never says who she is + my Aunt Ella + and she just launches straight into + whatever she's got to say + and she's halfway through it when it strikes you
               | who ++ | you're speaking to
               | A: who it is |

(2.14)   A: a friend + a stupid friend of mine got her telephone cut off + because well she asked for it to be cut off in fact + because her last bill was £500
            B: oh goodness + . . . oh that's dreadful
            A: she comes from Venezuela + of course that's these long distances + it's two or three pounds a time + maybe for a minute or two ++
            B: oh but imagine getting a bill into the house for that oh my goodness + that's the biggest one I've heard of + Mrs. Gibson got an awfully big one but she's been talking to Can + Canada a few times . . .

In everyday life this swapping of personal experiences constantly arises. Sometimes the matter is *transactional*, the details of what happened are important, and it matters that the listener gets the details correct. Obvious examples are news reports on radio and television, eye-witness accounts given to the police of burglaries, bank robberies etc., accounts given to insurance agents of domestic and traffic accidents, accounts given to magistrates by social workers of the misdemeanour of a truant, accounts given by patients to dentists of trouble with their teeth, accounts given by complaining customers to stores about an unsatisfactory electric appliance, accounts given by householders to the fire service of where exactly they live, and so on. One of the communicative skills which is a necessary component of normal social life is the ability to extract the relevant salient 'facts' from a mass of detail, and to communicate an event in terms of the structure imposed on it by the speaker.

Consider the ingredients of an event. An event takes place in a *setting*, over a particular *time* and something is required to *happen* in it. In interactional conversations the setting is not always explicitly mentioned because the nature of the event may presuppose a particular setting. 'I was watching TV last night' does not specify where I was watching it and, in the absence of any indication to the contrary, the listener will assume that the speaker was watching it where people usually watch it (i.e. at home). In transactional conversation this detail needs to be made explicit. Whereas in interactional conversation we assume a lot of shared knowledge and tend to be relatively inexplicit, in transactional conversation we assume much less, spell out much more, because it matters that the listener thoroughly understands what is being said. In this section we are concerned with transactional conversation, therefore, we will put a premium on explicitness.

Suppose a student has in front of him a set of cartoon pictures which depicts a series of events (a familiar EFL prompt). His listener has a jumbled pile of cartoon pictures which contain some which relate to this story, mixed up with others which don't. The job for the speaker is to tell the story in such a way that the listener can select the relevant pictures and arrange them in the right order. (In a more advanced class the listener may have to take notes on the series of events, or ask questions which elicit the sequence of events which leads up to the event portrayed in the last picture of the series, which is the only picture the listener/'investigator' can see.) Now the speaker has to extract from the series of cartoon pictures a structured event. This is not a *linguistic* task, but a cognitive task, which different individuals are more or less good at. It is important that the speaker really understands the story and the *point* of the story before beginning to speak. In working with cartoon sequences presented to native adolescents, we have observed a wide range of competence in appreciating what the artist intended in constructing a cartoon sequence. Quite divergent, even bizarre, stories are constructed by some students on the basis of the same standard input. This finding ought to lead us to a careful control of the use of cartoon sequences as prompts for language production. It is important that a student's *linguistic* competence is not confused with his ability to interpret a cartoon sequence.

Given that the student has understood the story, what information does he need to transfer to his listener? First he should give an indication of the setting – whether the scene is set indoors or outdoors, in a living room or in a restaurant, in a modern European town or in ancient Egypt. The amount of detail required in the description of the setting will vary depending upon the contribution of the setting to the story. If the pictures represent 'a night-time setting', and the story is about a burglary or someone becoming wildly intoxicated, then it is probably relevant to mention that it is evening/dark/night, etc. If no indication of time-of-day is given, and it is not relevant to the unfolding events, then it should not be mentioned. Similarly if the story is set in a living room, there is no reason to mention any pictures there may be conventionally shown on the walls, unless the point of the story is that the pictures are being stolen one by one, or that some character is obsessed by one of them. The selection of the relevant details of the setting demands a certain sophistication on the part of the speaker. For students from closely related cultural backgrounds, this may not prove a difficult problem. For students from very different cultural backgrounds, help and practice in the selection of features relevant to the story may need to be provided.

A great number of cultural assumptions which would be normally presupposed, and not made explicit by native speakers, may need to be drawn explicitly to the attention of speakers from other cultures. Thus, if two people are shown sitting in a room containing a settee and two easy chairs, and they are watching television, native speakers will tend to interpret this as showing the living room of the house which these two people habitually live in. If these two people are a man and a woman, and are middle-aged or elderly, then the assumption will be that they are a married couple. If later detail in the story made it clear that the two people were in fact in a dentist's waiting room, the artist might be claimed to have been misleading because British dentists' waiting rooms do not stereotypically contain televisions. Cartoons are governed by powerful stereotypes which reflect the culture they stem from. In foreign language teaching, they may play a valuable role as props which enable the teacher to establish those same stereotypes for the foreign learner. It is important to distinguish between the student's ability to recognise stereotypes, which relates to his knowledge of British background and culture, and his control of the appropriate language for describing them. If the student is to provide the appropriate language, it is essential that he recognises the stereotypes.

It is probable that the identification of the relevant features of the setting is made easier for the student if only relatively few features are depicted. The more detail, the more the conscientious student, who is unclear what is required, is likely to include. Moreover, the details which are included may be randomly selected, depending on whether or not the student happens to have available the name for some particular object which the artist happens to have represented as part of the background. If the exercise is 'name all the objects you recognise in this picture', the student who mentions all possible objects will score high. If all that is required is that he identify the relevant features of the setting, that selection demands a quite different sort of skill, which demands not only matching vocabulary items to objects, but determining which of the objects needs to be mentioned.

Let us suppose that the student has succeeded in providing an adequate, relevant, characterisation of the setting. Next, he must inform his listener who the participants in his narrative are. Once again there are obvious possibilities of grading the cognitive and the linguistic load here. If the speaker is to recount a story about a man and a woman, it is easy for him to identify the two individuals concerned as long as he controls the vocabulary items *man* and *woman*. He can re-refer to these individuals using the expressions *the man* and *the woman* or he can quite unambiguously use the pronouns *he* and *she*. In such a task it is relatively easy for the speaker to make it quite clear who he is talking about at any given moment. Indeed, it is possible to add a third participant, say a dog, and that participant hardly complicates the account because the dog can be unambiguously referred to by the expressions *the dog* and *it*. Consider the following example and note the ease with which it is possible to identify the participants referred to by pronouns (in italics):

(2.15)   there's a boy + erm with a catapult + *he*'s just turned round and *he* can see a + a fly + flying about + *he*'s turned round and *he*'s going to hit *it* with *his* catapult +

The referents of the expressions *he* and *it* and *his* are perfectly clear.

The task is immediately complicated if, instead of being a story about a boy and an insect, it is a story about two men. It is no longer adequate for the speaker to identify his participants with simple expressions like *a man* and *the man*. Now he has to distinguish between two individuals of the same sort, between *the old man* and *the young man*, or *the dark man* and *the fair man*, or *the man who is bald* and *the man with glasses*. The participants may differ along a number of different variables. The speaker has to choose a distinguishing feature for each individual and maintain that distinguishing feature. He has to make it clear which individual he is referring to at any one time.

Consider a story which first depicts an elderly woman sitting in a kitchen reading a book (a housewife), then moves to an event concerning a beautiful young girl in a mediaeval chamber (a princess) and then returns to the woman in the kitchen again. Here are some of the expressions which adolescent native speakers of English produced in telling this story:

(2.16)	*Housewife's introduction*	*Princess's introduction*	*Housewife's re-introduction*
A:	a woman	a princess	the woman
B:	a mother	a beautiful girl	the mother
C:	a woman	a woman	the woman
D:	a woman	a lady	the lady

Speakers A and B both produce descriptions which are adequate to distinguish between the two individuals. They characterise the individuals differently, using different vocabulary, but they succeed in distinguishing between them on first mention (*woman / princess, mother / beautiful young girl*) and in making it clear that the 'reintroduction' refers back to the first woman introduced rather than to the second. Speaker C fails to distinguish between the individuals. It is clear that the woman introduced is distinct from the first because she is introduced by the indefinite referring expression *a woman*, but it is quite unclear which of them the 'reintroduction' expression *the woman* refers to. Speaker D is positively misleading in this respect, since his 'reintroduction' expression *the lady* appears to refer back, not to the housewife, but to 'the princess', who he introduced with the expression *a lady*.

One problem with introducing two same-type participants into a story is that the speaker needs to maintain a consistent distinction between them. He has to be consistent in his use of lexical expression, as we saw in discussing the examples in extract (2.16); and he also has to be careful in his use of pronominal expressions, since here again a potential source of confusion exists. If the speaker uses pronominal expressions simply to refer back to the character he has immediately previously introduced, as in extract (2.17), no problems of reference arise.

(2.17)   there's a housewife who's bored with *her* everyday chores in the kitchen and + *she* dreams of how life could be for *her* + and *she* has a daydream

If, however, there are two competing female referents, as in the example we looked at in extract (2.16), there are dangers in using *she* as the 'reintroduction' expression:

(2.18)	E: this woman	this beautiful young woman	she
	F: this woman in her kitchen	a princess upstairs	she

In each case it is not clear which of the previously introduced women the expression *she* refers to. The tendency of native speakers will be to interpret the expression with respect to the immediately previously mentioned character, which, in both these cases, would be misleading.

The 'communicative stress' load, looked at from the point of cognitive difficulty, is increased as same-gender referents are included. Thus a story about a man and a woman is going to be easier, at the level of making clear who is doing what, than a story about a man with two girlfriends which, in turn, will be easier than the story of two men each of whom has a girlfriend. Even the most competent native speaker would find it hard to tell a story which involved two men, each of whom has two girlfriends, all of whom are separately involved in the action. It is clear that it is the cognitive load which is the complicating factor, rather than the linguistic forms. It is the ability to use language adequately which is at issue, rather than simply knowing the forms of the language.

This consideration may be relevant to those teachers who complain that beginners, who may be highly mature and intelligent individuals, are constantly frustrated by the boringly easy exercises they are invited to do. The implication is that, knowing so little language it must necessarily follow that the uses to which that language is put must be simple. It should be clear from our discussion of referentially easy tasks, as opposed to referentially more complex tasks, that this does not necessarily follow. It is only necessary for the student to control a trivially larger amount of vocabulary, sufficient to enable him to distinguish between the characters in the story, for him to be able to undertake what are cognitively far more demanding tasks. Whereas the linguistic forms known to an adult beginner and a twelve-year-old beginner may be very similar, the nature of the cognitive exercises in which they are asked to practise that language should obviously be pitched at very different levels. The adult has all the experience of using his own language competently, which ought to permit him to undertake the cognitively stressful task with little difficulty. The problems for him arise simply from not controlling the foreign language adequately. For the younger, immature, learner, the problems reside both in inadequate knowledge of the language *and* in the cognitive difficulty of the task.

So far we have merely considered problems arising from stating the relevant features of the setting, initially identifying the participants and maintaining the separate identity of the participants. (In chapter 4 we present a detailed discussion of how to assess relative success in doing this.) Other features of event-structure which may contribute to its relative ease or difficulty include whether or not the same setting is maintained throughout the story since, if the place changes, a new set of stereotypes needs to be called upon to determine what are the relevant features of the change of place and what are the implications of the change of place for the story. In one cartoon sequence we have worked with, a man and his wife are sitting together in their living room. The woman is sitting in an armchair, reading, and the man is sitting smoking. We next see the man standing in the hallway, looking in a mirror, straightening his tie. What is the significance of this change of scene? Why is the man in the hallway? Under what circumstances do men stereotypically straighten their ties? The next scene shows him in a bar. What assumptions do we make about this? We must assume that the sequence depicts the man moving from his living room (leaving his wife behind), getting ready to go out, shown in a hallway still in the same house, and going to a bar which will not be in his house (since British houses do not stereotypically contain bars with barmen and other drinkers) but which, we assume, will be in the same town, since we have not been told that he has flown, for example, to Las Vegas. We assume, moreover, that this change of place setting is also informing us about the structure of the temporal setting. We assume that these events happened in the order depicted, and that they all occurred close together in time, on the same evening, probably within the space of half-an-hour. The foreign learner, in order to interpret what is going on in this sequence of events, must be able to use the indications of place and their consequent indications of time, in the same way as the native speaker uses them.

There are, obviously, further possible complications arising in events represented in cartoon sequences. The sequence of temporal events may not occur in a simple succession, but involve flashbacks or simultaneous interpretation. The events themselves may be interpreted in the light of complex socio-cultural variables. Thus, in the cartoon story we have just been discussing, the wife sits up straight in her chair as she reads and looks satisfied with her lot in life. The husband, on the other hand, is slumped in his chair with a frown on his face. The conclusion that he is going out because he is bored at home may not be readily available to students from all cultures, but it constitutes an important ingredient of the speaker's ability to interpret what happens in the rest of the story, as the man meets a younger woman.

Sequences of events represented in cartoons demand considerable sophistication in their socio-cultural interpretation. They may very usefully be exploited by teachers to illustrate stereotypical features of British life and culture, which are essential to the interpretation of the cartoon representation. These are essential to the student's ability to interpret in language what is being pictorially represented. As we suggested in chapter 1, it seems more valuable for the teacher to use British background and culture courses to explore the socio-cultural stereotypes that lie behind the native speakers' use and interpretation of language, rather than to teach to the foreign learner details of the British Parliamentary system which native adolescents have rarely encountered. Whereas sequences of events represented in cartoons may be readily interpretable in western European cultures, they clearly ought to be used with great care among foreign learners generally.

An account of a sequence of events which is less socioculturally determined is the eye-witness account of a car crash. Here the speaker is required to give an account of a car crash to a listener who is taking the role of an insurance agent; the listener completes a diagram which indicates the setting (locality), the number and direction of cars, and their eventual positions vis-à-vis each other as they are engaged in an accident. The speaker may be presented with a series of photographs which show a number of cars as they approach each other. It is immediately obvious that the task of distinguishing between the participants is going to be difficult, because all of the participants will be same-gender. The simplest version of the task will be where two different vehicles (say a lorry and a bus) collide with each other on a straight road. An obviously much more difficult version of the task might include three cars colliding at a T-junction or a cross-roads. Once again the speaker will have to identify each of the cars uniquely as, for example, *the car with the light roof, the estate wagon, the Ford*, situate them within a setting, and then give an account of how they become mutually involved in the accident, making it quite clear which car is masking, hitting or running into which other car and at which point in time. This is a task which can be graded in terms of setting (straight road, junction, roundabout), participants involved (easier with *the lorry* than *the car with the light roof*), the number of participants, and the relative structuring of events in time (the more, the more difficult). It is possible to complete this type of task successfully with fairly limited vocabulary – sufficient to distinguish between the participating vehicles, to specify spatial and temporal relationships, and to describe the actions performed by the cars (*turn, come, go, crash*). The difficulty lies not so much in an extensive knowledge of

45

language as in the competent and flexible exploitation of fairly limited language to make it quite clear what is happening and who is doing what to whom. In chapter 4 we discuss the assessment of tasks of this kind.

Grading tasks: descriptions and instructions

In interactional conversation we frequently describe things to each other – other people, other people's houses, meals, clothes, books, films, household gadgets – not in a temporal structure, but in terms of their physical attributes as in (2.19).

(2.19)   (a) A: they were very dark houses +
                  B: very narrow windows and things too + +
                  A: very little ventilation + and substandard + +

    (b) well I have a friend + quite a well-educated lady she is + +

    (c) you've never had a Harvey Wallbanger + it's vodka galleano and fresh orange juice with lots of crushed ice + blows your head off +

    (d) we found erm + an Irish Bar in San Francisco that was famous for its Irish coffee + and they had a long bar it was about fifty feet long + with just rows and rows of glasses + +

    (e) along there I think second floor up + there was a big family of them + oh there must have been ten or twelve + and oh I can vividly remember going along there + in the kitchen there was a huge dresser + oh longer than this room is long + (really) a great big wooden dresser + +

These snippets from unstructured interactional conversation should serve to remind you of how frequently we do offer descriptions in normal life – often, of course, as part of the account of the setting for an anecdote as in (2.19d) above, where the speaker is going on to describe what happened in *the Irish Bar*.

Similarly, we often, in everyday life, tell someone else how to do something – where to find a shop, how to get from the hotel to the railway station, how to make a particular dish which a guest has just praised, how to draw a flow diagram, how to assemble a do-it-yourself kit, etc. Instructions have a lot in common with descriptions from the point of view of the language used, in that they frequently involve imposing a temporal structure upon a collection of objects which are not intrinsically temporally structured, and they often involve spatial relationships and the attribution of particular properties. Although instructions can be expressed using imperative forms, they are also often expressed in simple descriptive terms so (2.20a) below may be functionally equivalent to (2.20b) where the listener understands that he is receiving an instruction:

(2.20)   (a) put the rod diagonally across the switches
          (b) the rod is put diagonally across the switches

A reasonably realistic-looking task is to ask one student (who knows how to do it) to tell another (who doesn't) how to assemble a household object like the elderly mincer whose parts are displayed in illustration 5 (p. 154 below). This mincer consists of five essential parts which need to be identified and then put together in a correct order (which imposes a temporal sequence on the instructions) and in the appropriate spatial relationships, so that it matters, for instance, whether the flattened end or the rounded end of 'the screw-like object' protrudes from the narrow end of 'the gun-shaped object'.

Notice, first, that there is no 'correct vocabulary' for identifying the various pieces of the mincer. The foreign learner, like any native speaker, has to make do with what language he has available to try to distinguish between the pieces. (No doubt there are 'correct' technical terms available to the makers of the mincer, but these are not available to the general English-speaking public.) Rather than attempt to impose a rigid set of 'correct' terms here, the teacher would do better to provide interpretations of what the students would like to describe the particular piece as, in cases where the student is not able to provide a description for himself. Thus native speakers describe the smallest piece in various ways in (2.21).

(2.21)   (a) the smallest piece
          (b) the small star-shaped piece
          (c) this four-blade sort of propellor
          (d) the cross-shaped bit
          (e) a round bit in the middle with four little jaggy bits
               sticking out
          (f) the bit that's the blades
                                   etc.

This is an exercise in using language flexibly, not to come up with 'correct' vocabulary, but to come up with an adequate description which succeeds in identifying the piece the speaker wants to talk about. It exploits and extends his 'communicative competence'. Like the narrative sequences discussed in the last section, exercises of this kind can be graded. Fewer, simpler pieces with fewer, simpler interrelationships will be easier to describe than more complex pieces with more detailed and complex interrelationships. (Detailed assessment procedures for this type of task are discussed in chapter 4.)

The type of exercise that this particular task represents can be presented in many different formats. An obvious format is where one student describes to another how to draw a diagram which the first student.can see, but the second cannot see. The diagram may be simple, containing for example only two items with easily nameable properties in a simple spatial relationship. Thus it may contain a red square above a black circle. Here the two items need to be identified, together with their properties (colour and size), the relationship holding between them, and the placing on the page. It is very easy to imagine more complex diagrams, involving whole or partial overlapping, with each complex object being specified in terms of several different features (some complicated diagram types are described in chapter 4). 'Drawing a diagram' does not immediately present itself as the sort of task which most of us are required to do in everyday life. However, the skills required in describing a diagram for someone to draw are, of course, the very same skills which are required in instructing someone how to wire an electric plug or how to complete a wiring diagram, how to assemble a tent, or, indeed, how to assemble a complex chemical apparatus, or even a helicopter. In each case the speaker needs to be able to identify (verbally) the entity he is talking about, often identifying it in terms of its criterial properties, and then he needs to specify the spatial relations which this entity enters into with other entities – the more complex the relationships, the more difficult to describe adequately. The more similar the entities, the more difficult to distinguish adequately. In order to broaden the type of task to include technical instructions, it must be made clear that what is required is that the listener should produce a careful and *exact* copy of what the speaker is looking at.

In chapter 4 we discuss a range of descriptive and instructional tasks which are capable of evoking language which can be directly assessed. There are, of course, many types of task which a teacher can prepare, some of which will not evoke a sufficient amount of language to be worth considering as a basis for assessment, but which, nonetheless, would provide the student with practice in producing instructions and descriptions of many different sorts. It is clearly the case that students with different interests and from different cultural backgrounds will find some descriptive tasks more or less difficult, for cognitive rather than linguistic reasons. Suppose that a speaker has three photographs in front of him, each showing a different black-and-white cow. His listener has a copy of one of the photographs in front of him. The speaker has to describe each of his photographs so that the listener can determine which of the three he (the listener) is looking at. For a speaker–listener pair from a rural background who are used to considering the distinctive attributes of cows, this may prove a comfortable and relatively straightforward task. A pair from an urban background may engage in a totally unproductive hassle, which has little to do with their command of language, much more to do with their limited experience of cows. Many attractive-seeming exercises regularly fail to work satisfactorily because what is perceptually salient for the speaker in a pair is not perceptually salient for the listener. Description of the physical attributes of human beings, for instance, is often very misleading unless the distinctive physical characteristics are very gross indeed. Native speakers from the same background often find it problematical to describe one member of a group so that the listener can distinguish that individual from the rest of the group (a problem well known to teachers trying to identify a student, by description, to another teacher). A task which may look very straightforward to a course-designer because it involves, say, an individual who wears spectacles as opposed to others who do not, may turn out to be very difficult for an individual student who is tuned-in to nose-shapes, or beards or shirt colours, which in this case may happen not to be distinctive, and who simply does not appear to notice the spectacles which were thought to be so obvious. Since, among any group of students, there will be a wide range of interest in items which are capable of being described – clothes, cars, buildings, chess configurations, bridge hands, flowers, electronic games, figures in modern dance, diesel engines, kitchens, etc. – all of which can be found depicted in newspapers, magazines, colour supplements, technical journals – the students may fruitfully be asked to participate in developing their own exercises on topics which interest them. They can bring along gadgets, pictures, photographs, visuals cut out of newspapers, and decide on a 'task' for their listeners to do as they hear their descriptions. (Where speaker and listener agree that they have developed a good exercise, which has extended their ability to talk and understand in the foreign language, the teacher might profitably 'borrow' the format and add it to his own task-bank.) Students can thus begin to choose what it is they want to be able to talk about in the foreign language, to determine their own needs and interests.

The organisation of the spoken language production class may vary between tasks which are provided by the teacher, which determine the basic, graded, incremental course, and exercises provided by the students which enable them to talk about something that interests them in the foreign language. When the task is completed, the student pairs have the topic provided for them by the task to 'chat' about if they wish to, so the transactional task may be used as the basis for interactional conversation.

49

Teaching spoken production

A point we have not insisted on, but which must have become perfectly obvious, is that each task-based exercise of the kind we have described here, and will describe further in later chapters, not only provides practice in speaking for the speaker, but also provides practice in listening, for a purpose, for the listener.

Grading tasks: the discoursal approach

In the last few sections we have discussed in some detail some of the sorts of language use which involve longer turns, where the speaker has to take control of the structure of conversation for a while. We have concentrated on transactional language, where the speaker has some particular information which he wishes to transfer to a listener, who needs that information in order to complete some specified task; and we have suggested that in transactional situations the *accuracy* of information-transmission is at a premium.

We have suggested, moreover, that in this aspect of teaching the spoken language the teacher can deliberately select the level of difficulty that he wishes his students to be able to cope with, and train them to that level of ability. He can analyse the linguistic requirements that a particular type of task puts upon the speaker, as well as the cognitive demands, and he can produce a course which enables the speaker to learn the necessary linguistic skills in the context in which he needs those skills.

This approach demands that the teacher becomes much more aware of how discourse in spoken language is produced, and how long turns are structured. The teacher must observe not only sentence structures which have traditionally been the concern of 'short turn' approaches, but how native speakers inventively and flexibly use the language to cope with the demands of the communicative situation. We shall discuss just one aspect here of the sort of discoursal control which the foreign learner, like the native speaker, will be expected to produce.

We have commented, in all the tasks we have so far discussed, on the requirement that a speaker not only identify individuals as he introduces them into the discussion, but maintain discrete reference to each individual. We have talked of the difficulties some speakers have in making it clear when a character is reintroduced into a narrative (*the housewife, the princess, she*) and we discussed the problem for the speaker in discriminating between a number of same-gender referents in the eye-witness account of car crashes, particularly where more than two cars are involved. The same problem arises in descriptive tasks, for example a diagram-describing task, where two or more same-gender objects (say triangles) are involved. As we have suggested, the student a) has to maintain the same description of the entity and b) has only to use a pronominal form when it is quite clear which entity the pronoun refers to.

Let us consider the requirements of a) first, as applied to a car crash task. In the examples below, the expressions for first and second mention of the same referent are shown:

(2.22)   A: 1. there's a car coming from the right . . .
          2. the car coming from the right . . .

          B: 1. there were two cars coming from the right . . .
          2. the two cars on the right . . .

          C: 1. there's one car coming from the right . . .
          2. the car that came from the right . . .

All these speakers succeed in maintaining the same description of the relevant car(s) when they introduce it for the second time. The following speakers have a much less successful strategy:

(2.23)   A: 1. a car's going along the road . . .
          2. the car coming down . . .

          B: 1. there's two cars coming one way . . .
          2. the car at the top . . .

          C: 1. there were two cars on one side of the road . . .
          2. the car that came straight along . . .

Since speaker A in (2.23) already has a further moving car in his description, it cannot be clear to the listener that *the car coming down* is identical to *the car going along the road*. Neither speaker B nor speaker C gives any indication in his first description which will enable the listener to know which of the two cars is being referred to when they are next mentioned. In chapter 4 we examine the implications of this in assessment.

Let us now consider the problems which arise with the inadequate use of pronominal forms. Here is another car crash description:

(2.24)   the second car + hasn't got time to avoid + the car which tried + which + swerved away to avoid the car which was pulling out + and he hits *it*

(It is a noticeable feature of native speaker descriptions that they frequently endow the model cars engaged in mock accidents with *drivers* – and indeed endow those drivers with properties as in the comment 'he's a speed merchant'.) See illustrations 8 and 9, pp. 157, 158 below. The problem here is what *it* is referring to – is it *the car which swerved away* or is it *the car which was pulling out*? There are two possible interpretations here and a real problem for the insurance agent who does not know which car was hit in this incident.

One desperate remedy to adopt would be to advise students never to use pronominal forms when there are two competing same-gender referents. A very stilted sort of English would result from this. It would be much better for students to adopt a strategy used by native speakers who are generally successful in this task. Consider the following extracts:

(2.25)   (a) there was a car approaching a T-junction and *it* was going quite fast
                (b) there's another car coming and *it*'s supposed to stop + but *it* doesn't stop

The speakers here safely use *it* to refer back to the last-mentioned car. However, when another car is introduced into the discussion, successful speakers reintroduce this other car with a full noun phrase and accompanying description (e.g. *the car with a light roof*). One 'safe' strategy to operate appears to be that you only use pronominal forms to refer back to the last-mentioned participant. As soon as a new participant is introduced, any pronominal form will now refer back to that new participant, until some even newer participant is introduced. This might form the basis for initial pronominal practice.

However, there is at least one other strategy for pronominal use which native speakers rely on. This strategy demands that the speaker selects one particular topic-participant and he relates everything else that happens to his particular topic-participant. He adopts a 'point of view' for his account. In the case of a complex car accident, for example, he would recount what happened from the point of view of one of the cars as the speaker in the following extract does:

(2.26)   the two cars were waiting at the right-hand side junction – waiting to come in + *the car at the front* decided to pull out not seeing the car overtaking from behind + then as *it* came out from the junction + *it* saw the other two cars + *it* hit the first one which then collided with the one overtaking +

(Note that, although the speaker is describing 'cars', those cars can 'decide' and 'see'. We shall reconsider this assumption that cars must have drivers in chapter 3.)

The point we have made in this section is that successful *teaching* of discoursal competence demands of the teacher that he should analyse the language which native speakers use in discourse, in order that he can ensure that reasonable and realistic models are presented for his students to imitate and base their own performances on.

In producing discourse of the sort we have been discussing in this chapter, we are assuming that the discoursal strategies of taking long structured turns which the speaker uses to describe, narrate, instruct etc. are all strategies which are available to him in his native language. We are assuming that it is not the job of the foreign language teacher to teach those basic skills. Rather it is the teacher's job to provide the student with the necessary language to make those skills work in English. (Mother-tongue teachers, on the other hand, will often find they need to train these skills explicitly.)

Pronunciation and intonation

We have not paid attention in this book to the teaching of pronunciation and intonation. This is partly because our aim here is to focus on developing the student's ability to use English to communicate with someone in long transactional turns, an ability which we believe has been relatively neglected in recent developments in EFL. When a student is trying to formulate and structure a long turn in a foreign language, the last thing a teacher should be thinking of is correcting that student's pronunciation or intonation. In this stressful task the student needs all the support he can get from the teacher, not criticism of relatively extraneous features like pronunciation. Just as it is unhelpful to a student who has written a good essay to find that the teacher, rather than being pleased with him, has nothing better to comment on than his poor handwriting, so a student who is working at organising what he wants to say, who will necessarily not be paying full attention to how he is articulating it, should not be distracted from the *point* of the exercise by comments on the way he is pronouncing what he is saying.

It is very hard for teachers, especially those particularly interested in pronunciation, to hear a student consistently making a pronunciation error. If this occurs, the teacher should note the error (along with other segmental and suprasegmental problems) and deal with it separately, after the task the student is concerned with is completed. When the point is to develop fluency in 'self-expression' in the spoken language, few things are more inhibiting than being constantly corrected. If it is quite unclear what the student is saying, the person who should be asking for clarification is the interlocutor, the listener, not the teacher. In practice sessions (as opposed to an assessment session), the listener should be permitted, indeed encouraged, to ask questions of clarification, just as native speakers do in normal life. If the listener can make sense of what the speaker is saying, then the speaker is, on this occasion, communicating successfully. (For discussion of pronunciation teaching and intonation teaching, see the list of references at the end of the book.)

3 Teaching listening comprehension

3.0 'Listening comprehension ought to be naturally acquired'

In the last ten years listening comprehension has begun to be taken
seriously. Previously, where there was any interest at all, it seemed
to be assumed that the student would just pick it up somehow in
the general process of learning the foreign language. It seemed
reasonable to assume that he would learn to understand it as he
learnt to speak it and, anyway, he would of course understand the
language addressed to him by his teacher.

Sadly, this apparently natural process doesn't seem to produce the
desired results. There are a number of possible reasons for this. One
is that the student is taught to speak slowly and clearly and his
teacher generally addresses the class in a public style (sometimes in a
caricature 'speaking to foreigners, the stupid or the deaf' style) which
is also slow and clear. Native speakers, much of the time, don't speak
slowly or particularly clearly. Moreover, the student is often only
exposed to one accent of English, usually only that spoken by his
teacher and *as* spoken only by his teacher. The normal habits of
simplification which characterise the accent may be lost when the
teacher speaks slowly and 'artificially' clearly. Students consequently
get used to a model of speech where every segment is clearly articulated. Normal native English speakers have habitual patterns of
simplification in speech which vary somewhat from individual to
individual, and vary considerably between accents. Listen to extracts
(3.1) and (3.2) on the tape. The first speaker is an RP (standard
southern English) speaker, describing a rainbow.

(3.1) (2) |an actual bow|+ an arc + right over the sky + +
             | [ən ˈakʃəl] |

             which has got +|different colours|erm|+ +
                            | [dɪfrən ˈkʌləz] | |

             |can't remember what|they are but they're . . .
             |[kɑ̃ ˈtrɪmwɒt] |

The transcription draws attention to some of the details of her speech
which is simplified following fairly general RP habits in the first two

54

phrases (loss of [t] between [k–ʃ] in *actual*, loss of [t] between [n–k] in *different colours*), but simplited in an idiosyncratic way in her production of *can't remember what*, where a good deal of *remember* disappears altogether. Consider now the second speaker (from northern USA, also describing a rainbow):

(3.2) (3)   you|usually|see a|rainbow|+ uh + when it's raining +
            |[juʒəli]| |[rēibou]|

or|just before|or|just after it|rains +|when the sun|
  |[dʒəsbɪˈfor]| |[dʒəstaftr]| |[wən?əˈsʌn]|

comes out ++ so ++ after it rains ++ uh ++ and you
see something in the sky – that's|red – and green and blue|
                                  |[ˈred+nːˈgrinən ˈblu]|

((hm) laughter) . . .

Note the nasalisation replacing the [n] in *rainbow* and the way 'just' loses its [t] when it occurs before a consonant (*just before*), but retains it when it occurs before a vowel (*just after*), that it's not clear that there is any [ə] in the phrase *when the sun* (which might, then, have been transcribed as *when a sun*) and that the word *and* is realised in different ways on different occasions once as [nː] and once as [ən]. The type of simplification illustrated here is very common in normal speech, much denser than is usually supposed (cf. list of references at the end of the book for literature dealing with this phenomenon). It will necessarily provide the student with an unfamiliar input and cause him the same sorts of difficulties that unfamiliar types of handwriting pose for all of us when we have only been trained to read printed texts in the foreign language.

The impression of unfamiliar input will, of course, be reinforced for the student if he has been used to hearing clearly articulated *sentences* in the target language, and suddenly has to cope with the 'make it up as you go along', phrase-by-phrase, spoken language produced by normal speakers, as in extracts (3.1) and (3.2).

Most foreign learners will not acquire a comfortable ability to listen and understand the foreign language as spoken by native speakers if they only listen to their teacher and classmates and feedback from their own spoken production.

3.1 Teaching listening comprehension

If the ability to understand the spoken form of the foreign language is not acquired naturally, then it appears obvious that this ability must be taught. Consequently classes on listening comprehension are introduced into many curricula and what began as a trickle, but is now a flood, of courses in listening comprehension are available on the market.

Most of these courses are structured in the same way. They typically contain chunks of spoken language which take between three and seven minutes to play. The playing of the tape is sometimes intended to be prefaced with some remarks on its content and, occasionally, by explanation of some 'difficult' vocabulary items which will be encountered in the text. The students are then expected to listen to the tape (sometimes twice). It is normally the case that they are then required to answer a series of questions on the factual content of the text. Often these questions are presented as multi-choice questions. In some cases the student has a written transcript of the text which he can refer to. In others he is expected to remember what it is that he has heard. The questions are typically evenly distributed throughout the text, usually at intervals which correspond to every three or four lines of a written transcript of the tape.

This type of presentation has, of course, for fifty years or more, been the standard presentation for written comprehension exercises. If it works for written comprehension exercises – and most students do eventually learn to understand at least simple written texts – why should it not work equally well for spoken language comprehension? We shall spend the rest of this chapter in attempting to answer this question, and in attempting to replace this view of teaching listening comprehension (which to an impartial observer might look rather more like 'testing' than 'teaching') with one which pays closer attention to the native speaker's experience of spoken language.

Before considering this question in detail, let us first establish some explicit definitions of key terms which we shall use. When we talk of the 'meaning' of an utterance, we could be referring to the *literal meaning* of the words combined in a particular structure. We could also be referring to what the speaker intended to convey by uttering those words, that is, the *speaker's intended meaning*. Since it has to be this latter type of meaning which we wish to grasp when we hear an utterance, the discussion which follows will be devoted to the 'comprehension' of utterances in terms of understanding what the speaker intended to convey. A distinction in terminology arises in connection with this distinction in types of meaning. 'Literal meaning' is clearly related to which 'words' are actually uttered. It is based on the *text* of what is said. If you write down a 'verbal record' of a piece of speech, you have produced a text of the utterances involved. If you wish to talk about 'speaker's intended meaning', you will rely to some extent on the words uttered, but you will also need to take many aspects of the context into consideration. When both 'text' and 'context' are considered together in terms of the interpretation of utterances, we shall use the term *discourse*. Discourse is text interpreted in context.

The distinction between 'literal meaning' and 'speaker's intended meaning' must be kept in mind when the notion of listening comprehension is considered. It is absurd to think that speakers will present, in words, everything they intend to communicate. Speakers have to be able to expect that their listeners will have some background knowledge of the way the world is and be capable of making reasonable inferences on the basis of this knowledge. Thus, when a listener encounters an utterance like:

(3.3)   the car turned round the corner and he couldn't see what was coming

there is no literal assertion of the fact that this car had a driver. In order to understand who *he* is, the listener has to 'fill in' this gap in the literal message. In so doing, the listener is constructing his interpretation of what the speaker intended to convey.

The listener may, of course, arrive at a wrong interpretation. In the example quoted, the speaker may have been talking about some man (*he*) who was about to cross the road. If the speaker intended the listener to arrive at this interpretation, then the need for an inference or a certain amount of interpretive 'work' on the listener's part is even more apparent.

If we remain aware of this process of understanding what we hear as a process of arriving at *a reasonable interpretation* of what the speaker intended to communicate, we can avoid the dangers of treating 'comprehension' as a 100 per cent notion. What native listeners operate with are partial, reasonable, interpretations of what they are listening to, and it seems unjustifiable to require of non-native listeners that they do more. Since it is presumably the general experience of success in understanding via such partial interpretations that allows the native listener to have confidence in his ability to understand what he hears (without, in any sense, totally comprehending everything he hears), then it should be this experience which we should provide for non-native listeners. That is, the aim of a listening comprehension exercise should be for the student to arrive successfully at a reasonable interpretation, and not process every word, and not to try to work out *all* that is involved in the literal meaning of the utterance, since that is, in principle, an impossible task.

3.2 What might 'listening comprehension' mean?

What does it mean to understand something that somebody has said to you? In EFL teaching it often seems that it is taken to mean that the listener can repeat the text. That is, if he could actually learn the text as he heard it, he would probably be said to have understood it. He could then demonstrate this understanding by matching chunks of the text he has learned to questions which contain part of the text and require the addition of the immediately preceding or following piece of text to answer them. This is the requirement of many multi-choice questions. A further requirement of understanding might be that the student should have heard and understood the meaning of particular vocabulary items as they are used in that text. A further requirement which is sometimes made is that the student should be able to resolve anaphoric reference and to determine which male character, previously mentioned, a particular expression, *he*, refers to. Some particularly sophisticated recent courses have introduced question types which demand that the student should be able to work out not only what is directly asserted in the text, but also what is implied.

What does it mean for a native speaker to have understood what someone has said to him? As soon as you start thinking about this question seriously you find that you want to introduce some hedges. You begin to say 'well, it depends what you mean by *understand*' and 'obviously it's different on different occasions'. You draw a distinction between what it might mean to answer this question with respect to someone who has just listened to the whole of *King Lear* on the radio, as opposed to someone who has just heard his father bellow 'shut the door' at him. Even in the second, apparently simple, case, you might conclude that there are probably different kinds of understanding involved. On the one hand the listener may under-stand the literal, verbally expressed, message that it is required of him that he shut the door. On the other hand the listener may understand that the message is produced in the way it is (i.e. bellowed), rather than uttered politely, because the father is irritated since his son has already failed to shut the door eight times that morning (i.e. the irritation is explicitly addressed to his son) or because he is having difficulty working out his mortgage repayments (i.e. is suffering a generalised irritation of which his son is a com-paratively innocent victim). In the first case the son may under-stand not only that he must shut the door behind him on this particular occasion, but also that he had better shut the door behind him on future occasions if he is to escape the paternal fury. In the second case the son may understand not only that he must shut the door on this occasion, but also that he would be well advised to assume a rather low profile until his father's irritation disappears, in particular not to interrupt him again while he is working. The son who 'understands' a normally uttered request to close the door in exactly the same way as he understands a bellowed instruction is going to have a hard time with social interaction and has probably missed the main point of the message. As normal human interactants we tend to operate with Sacks' procedural question, 'Why this, to me, now', and to interpret the 'this' in the light of the existing circumstances and the intentions we attribute to the speaker. The son in our example has not only to understand the verbal message, but to understand it *in the context in which it occurs*.

Our normal experience of spoken language involves us in interaction with speakers in more-or-less familiar contexts of situation. It is within such constraints that we learn to understand the native spoken language. The multitude of possible interpretations of every utterance we hear does not even occur to us, since the meanings we extract are so constrained by the context of utterance. As normal language interactants we can never be *sure* that we have thoroughly understood what a speaker said and, if he said a lot (as in a lecture), we may be pretty sure that we have failed to understand a good deal that he said. Our common experience must surely be that a speaker exposes some of his intentions in uttering language and achieves understanding by his listeners of only some of those intentions. We achieve a *partial* interaction of point of view, a *partial* understanding of what the speaker intended, most of the time. You may have perfectly understood the language of this paragraph but have you perfectly understood the point we are trying to make? ('Trying to make' indicates the problem.)

In spite of the fact that we are used to achieving only partial success with our own utterances and can only expect a partial understanding of much of the language that is addressed to us, nonetheless we clearly operate with the expectation of a tolerable degree of mutual comprehension, the habit of a tolerable degree of mutual comprehension. It is surely this expectation, this habit, of *tolerable* mutual comprehension which we wish to develop in our students.

It should follow from this that we should not train our students to expect that they ought to be achieving 100 per cent correct comprehension and that they are failing if they fail to achieve 100 per cent correct comprehension. A student trained in such expectations constantly experiences panic as he practises listening. He expects not to understand, since he has so often failed to in the past, and he stops trying to understand as soon as he fails to recognise a word or expression. He makes unreasonable hypotheses about what foreign language speakers might say, since they clearly achieve a perfection of expression which he is unused to in his native language – a perfection represented in marking schemes which enable the teacher to assign 100 per cent 'right' or 'wrong' assessments of his attempts to interpret. He keeps on trying to work out *after the event* what the speaker was saying, to work out *exactly* what the speaker said, in the sense of trying to recall 'the right words'. He is not helped in this panic by having the teacher introduce difficult vocabulary before he listens to the tape, often in terms which he finds difficult to understand. He is not helped by being forced into one of a number of different responses where several of them seem to him partly true. He is not helped by being required to listen to points at equal intervals of time, since very few speakers structure their content evenly like this, which means he sometimes , arbitrarily, has to pay attention to major points, but often, arbitrarily, to very minor points. It is hard to see that the student is being *taught* any particular skill in such a class. What weaker students inevitably and rapidly learn is that they are weak in listening comprehension in the foreign language.

We might claim that they are often being asked to perform tasks which native speakers of the language would have considerable difficulty with. They are being asked to treat the spoken language as if it were written language. They are being asked to ignore differences in form and function between interactional and transactional language, and to treat all spoken language as if it were primarily intended for the transference of facts. They are being asked to listen with a sustained level of attention, over several minutes, to spoken language, to interpret *all of it*, and to commit that interpretation, *all of it*, to memory, in order to answer random, unmotivated, questions on any of it. Few normal adult speakers can provide that level of sustained attention, interpretation, and committing to memory, even in their own language, for more than a minute or so.

3.3 Native listening: context and co-text

Compare the classroom situation of the foreign learner as we have just described it (you may think we have caricatured it but it is sadly the case that this still seems to represent the norm) with the experience of the native speaker in encountering spoken language.

The native speaker normally encounters spoken language, as we have already suggested, in a context of situation. He encounters that context with a set of stereotypical knowledge which he has been building up from the time he first acquired language as an infant in the culture. He is predisposed to construct expectations on the basis of this stereotypical knowledge. We shall discuss this stereotypical knowledge in terms of *speaker, listener, place, time, genre, topic* and *co-text*:

1 *Speaker*. The native listener generalises over his previous experience of listeners and constructs expectations on the basis of his experience of previous speakers who have been similar to this speaker in some respects. He will bring to his interpretation of what is said knowledge of what speakers of this kind (young / old, male / female, fat / thin, well-educated / ill-educated, beautiful / ugly, cheerful / cross, Yorkshire / London, etc.) playing this sort of role (prime minister, doctor, docker, father, gardener, knowledgeable man-of-affairs, career woman, person-at-a-bus-stop, naughty child, trade union leader, minister of religion, policeman, shopkeeper, experimental subject, car-salesman, nurse) are likely to say, given that he has knowledge of the rest of the features of situation. He will make judgments about the speaker's attitude (pleased / kind / courteous, etc.) and about what he assumes to be his intentions in speaking. The listener will interpret expressions like *I, me, myself* as referring to the speaker and will interpret expressions like *we, us, ours* as including the speaker but, depending on the context of situation, in particular on the *role* the speaker adopts in speaking, as intended to include 'me-and-you', 'me-and-you-and-others', 'me-and-my-family', 'me-and-my colleagues', etc.

2 *Listener*. On many occasions the speaker may be directly addressing the particular listener whose situation we are considering. The listener then knows from experience what sort of language this sort of speaker addressed to him. Sometimes, however, he listens to language which is not addressed to him. He functions as an *overhearer*. On such occasions he will have expectations of the sort of thing the speaker, in his role, will address to a listener, in his role. Thus two colleagues at a formal meeting may address each other by their titles and discuss relevant business, but meeting at home may address each other by first names and range over a much wider variety of topics.

3 *Place*. Our listener will expect to experience different language in different situations. One of the determinants of situation is the *place* where the talking goes on. There are some types of place where we have strong stereotypes of the sort of language that is appropriate (Parliament, law courts, doctors' surgeries, post offices, classrooms, Saville Row tailors, Air Force briefing rooms, operating theatres, bed, casinos, etc.). Of course our listener is aware that *any* sort of language can be produced in any place, but

nonetheless he has stereotypical norms of *appropriateness* which lead him to expect that language will be used in one way rather than another, depending on where it occurs. Our listener will interpret expressions like *here, there, this, come, fetch, in front of, to the left-hand side of*, in terms of the location of the speaker and the point of view the speaker adopts.

4 *Time*. We have stereotypical expectations deriving from temporal structure – from the beginnings and ends of stories, jokes, conversations, meetings, as well as from how the time of speaking relates to the time that is being spoken of – is it in the past, happening now, being anticipated in the future, etc.
Our listener will interpret expressions like *now, then, a year ago, this morning, next Tuesday, after that*, as well as tense forms in tensed sentences, in terms of the time of speaking. If the speaker locates an event at a particular point in time *during the war, when I was at school, during the Turkish occupation, when my sister was little*, the listener will have stereotypical expectations deriving from an intersection of his knowledge of the speaker, his purpose in speaking, the topic, and the time he is speaking of.

5 *Genre*. The listener will derive expectations from his experience of the sort of things that language is used for, and his identification of the particular event he is experiencing as one of these events – an informal chat, a news report, a formal warning, an anecdote, a debate, a lecture. He may identify a large-scale generic event – 'a church service' – and within that locate a small-scale generic event – 'a prayer' – and within that a micro-event – 'a vocative expression'. 'Experience of genre' includes experience of previous similar texts, of previous similar uses of language. The notion of 'appropriateness' derives particularly clearly from the notion of 'appropriate in a genre'. Previous experience, in language as in life in general, leaves us with 'some idea of what to expect'.

6 *Topic*. We shall use the notion rather loosely to mean 'whatever it is that is being talked about'. It is the topic which, to a large extent, determines the vocabulary which is selected. If the topic is concerned with the fact that X has just had a baby, then the vocabulary will include things that have to do with babies and having babies. Depending on whether the listener is a doctor or a friend, X is likely to be discussing different aspects of babies. If the topic is concerned with how to repair a bicycle tyre, the vocabulary selected will be that which is relevant to bicycle tyres. If the topic is primary school education, the vocabulary selected will, again, be influenced by this.

In some topic areas there are peculiar structures of argumentation which are characteristic of that topic, or subject area.

7 *Co-text.* The listener's expectation may be *globally* determined by the features of context which we have already described. They will be *locally* determined by whatever has already been said in a particular event. Thus if a speaker is telling our listener about how his elderly crippled mother finds it difficult to travel by train but has just been on a train journey to Rumania and embarks on an anecdote about his mother's adventures, the listener will expect to hear about adventures which could occur to an elderly lady travelling by train to Rumania. If a speaker makes an initial comment: 'I really think *The Times* is taking the strangest line on the Falklands', the listener will expect to hear an example of what the speaker is talking about. He would be surprised if the speaker went on to say, giving no indication of topic-change, 'It's reported "sun in Malaga" for the whole of last week.'

In most normal face-to-face interactions, the listener has access to information about the features of context we have mentioned. Not only does he have access to the information, he can relate that information to his previous experience. In interpreting the language which he hears he operates with two basic principles:

A.   *The principle of analogy.* This principle instructs us to expect that things will be as they were before. It is a principle which we assume in our normal conduct of life. We assume that doors will open, legs will bend, cats will purr, houses will stand, cars will start, pianos will play, until something goes wrong and they fail to. Most of our everyday behaviour is predicated on the expectation that all our habitual movements, actions, language, will operate as usual. Our normal expectation is that we do not have to pay attention to habitual, individual movements or actions, and that they can take place at some sub-conscious level, while we pay attention to, look out for, things which may be different, which may need conscious decision making (or, if we don't pay attention to the exterior world, we construct an absorbing interior world). Karl Popper asserts this fundamental human process: 'we are born with expectations . . .. One of the most important of these expectations is the expectation of finding a regularity. It is connected with an inborn propensity to look out for regularities, or with a need to *find* regularities.'

The second principle informs us what to expect when we are forced to admit that the first principle is not applying – when the door fails to open or the car won't start or the ear fails to hear:

B.   *The principle of minimal change.* This principle instructs us to assume that things are as like as possible to how they were before. This principle leads us to assume that the door won't open because it is stuck or locked, rather than that the door has been bricked up; that the car won't start because the battery is flat, rather than that someone has carted away the entire engine; that the ear fails to hear because of some local defect, rather than that someone has removed it totally. If you live in a culture or environment where it is normal to find the entire engine missing from your car, your notion of 'minimal change' will differ from that of people who live in cultures where this is a rare event. The principle will still operate, even if the interpretation may vary somewhat between cultures, and indeed between individuals. Many of us are familiar with individuals who lead peculiarly dramatic lives in which they always 'expect the worst'. These individuals are memorable precisely because most of us operate with far more limited expectations – we set our limits of 'as like as possible to how they were before' closer to our analogical paradigm – or perhaps we merely have more mundane experiences.

We operate with these two fundamental principles in our processing of language, just as we do with life in general. We assume that a speaker known to us will behave in the way he has behaved before – that he will be equally friendly, kind or critical, that he will maintain the same sort of views on the same range of topics, that he will behave in a manner consistent with the mental image we have of him. From time to time a speaker's mood may vary, his interests may change, but we will attempt to interpret his behaviour in the light of previous experience, adding the limited new information as accretions to the established information. We have similar expectations of all of the features of context of situation we have discussed.

Within a discourse we interpret the language in terms of the same set of constraints. We assume that the same time, the same place, the same topic, are all relevant unless the speaker explicitly marks them as having changed. If we did not operate within such expectations it is hard to see how we could interpret language like the following:

(3.4) A: I remember very vaguely but when the first man landed on the moon + +

B: mhm + +

A: my mother was saying + + sit and watch this + + this is history + +

B: oh + yes it was history right enough and

A: and my grandmother was there + my father's mother was there at the time + and she was just sitting there and saying + and that's somebody on the moon + I can look here at someone

B: I know

A: and she used to sit and think + oh +

B: it really is wonderful

A: I can't understand it

A, a young woman in her early twenties, has been talking to her elderly cousin, B, about wonderful modern inventions which have changed their experience of life. She begins by indicating that she is about to tell an anecdote, *I remember* (genre), which she only remembers *very vaguely* which suggests that the events she recounts took place quite a long time ago. She locates the point in time, *when the first man landed on the moon*, from which her listener could work out that the speaker must have been a child at the time she is speaking of. She goes on *my mother was saying + + sit and watch this*. The listener has to work out the context in which a mother might say *sit and watch* to her daughter, and from her stereotypical background knowledge derived from previous experience will presumably assume that the incident took place in her own home (which is where 'mothers' typically are) and that the daughter was told to watch television. What is it that is referred to by the expression *this*? We assume it is still what she was talking about before, *when the first man landed on the moon*. We assume that the expression *this is history* still refers to the same topic and is still to be understood as spoken by the same speaker to the same listener at the same time and in the same place. When A continues in her next turn *and my grandmother was there*, the listener will assume this is still the same time and the same place and that the grandmother's being there will somehow be related to the same topic. There are very powerful expectations in our interpretive processes which constrain our interpretation, but which we rarely bring to consciousness.

Consider a further example of these same processes at work. In chapter 2 we considered the constraints which members of a particular culture may operate with in interpreting the events represented in a series of cartoon drawings. Naturally those are the very same constraints which are applied when the listener interprets the language produced by someone who is giving an account of such a set of cartoons. How is the listener who has not seen the cartoons to interpret the language in extract (3.5)?

(3.5) (a)   a man and a woman sitting in the living room + the woman sitting reading quite happily – the man's bored goes to the window looks out of the window + and gets himself ready and goes out

The listener must interpret *the woman sitting reading quite happily* as the same woman he has just heard mentioned, so must construct an interpretation of this woman as 'sitting reading quite happily *in the living room*'. Similarly *the window* which the man goes to will be interpreted as 'the window in that same living room' since the listener will interpret events as taking place in the same place, unless he is told that the place is to change. In the next utterance *and goes out*, the listener is warned that the location may change if the story follows the fortunes of the man rather than staying with his wife. The speaker continues:

(3.5) (b)   goes to his goes to a club + has a drink talks to the barman + then he starts dancing with a beautiful girl – long black hair + has a good time +

The listeners will assume that the man (the same man – the same topic) *goes to a club* in the same town and on the same evening – minimal change. He will assume that *the barman* is the barman in the club. He will assume that it is in the same club and on the same occasion within a reasonably minimal time-span (e.g. not over a year) that he dances with the 'beautiful girl'. We assume that it is the 'beautiful girl' who has *long black hair*, that it is the 'same man' who on this 'same occasion' *has a good time*, etc.

It seems reasonable to suggest that principles of the sort we have been discussing are fundamental in human behaviour and must be, therefore, fundamental in the processing of language across cultures. Without doubt the principle of minimal change may be somewhat differently interpreted in different cultures, as we have already suggested. It must be the case, however, that all foreign learners are accustomed to relying on such procedures of interpretation in interpreting their own mother tongue.

So far we have called on the context of situation and, in particular, the co-text to account for the fact that, as language processors, our expectations of what may be said in a particular context by a particular speaker are narrowed down by our previous experience. We come to a particular speech event in a context of situation with expectations which limit our interpretations. The effect of context may be represented as in figure 3.1:

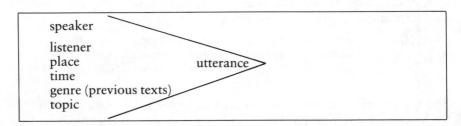

Figure 3.1   *Features of context limit expectations of the utterance content*

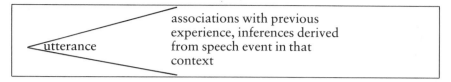

Figure 3.2   *Expansion of listener's model as a result of the utterance*

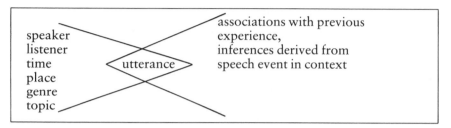

Figure 3.3   *Updating the listener's model*

It is important to note that this represents only part of what goes on in interpreting language in context. The listener's expectations may be generally activated so that he has global expectations of what is likely to be said. However, it is clearly the case that it is only in very rare instances that the context is so constrained that it permits prediction of the actual words which will be used. We can think of relatively few examples of 100 per cent prediction: the words written on British taps over washbasins, 'PUSH / PULL' on swing doors, 'ON / OFF' on switches. In the spoken language such 100 per cent prediction seems to be limited to rituals like religious services, legal observances, the opening of formal committee meetings, and so on. (Even here there is still room for creativity in language. One of us heard the following words uttered in a Ghanaian marriage service: 'those whom God hath joined together let no man + *nor no woman neither* + put asunder', which created a quite startling rhetorical effect as a departure from the expected norm.)

The effect of knowledge of the context will be to limit the listener's global expectations so that his relevant experience is activated as he approaches the speech event. He will have expectations about the sort of thing that might be said, in the sense that, even if he has no prior knowledge of the topic to be discussed, he will have some expectation of the kind of topic which is likely to be discussed by chemical engineers at a professional meeting, or between a traffic warden and a motorist who has just been booked for illegal parking.

He will have expectations of the type of opinion which is likely to be put forward, the type of attitude which the speaker may express. He will have expectations about the intentions, purposes, of the speakers in speaking, which will limit his interpretation in that context. (He may of course get it wrong – all of us sometimes do. Our experience, however, is of tolerable success.)

The effect of hearing and interpreting the first utterance in a speech event will be to establish the probable area of topic, which will yet further narrow down the listener's expectations. (It may set up a place / time dimension other than that of the speech event the listener is participating in. So if the speaker says 'On my way to work this morning . . .', the listener has to construct an appropriate time / place context.) Experiencing a particular utterance in a context yet further constrains the listener's expectation of what the following utterances are likely to contain. Simultaneously, however, the experiencing of an utterance in a context also enlarges the listener's expectations within that narrowed-down context. This expansion is represented in figure 3.2. A metaphor may help here. Suppose you are looking through the view-finder of a camera. From all the visual field which is available to you, you may select a small area, bounded by a view-finder, which you wish to pay attention to. We shall suggest that the effect of context on global expectation is like that selection of a limited area in your field of vision. Suppose now, having determined your area of interest, you take a zoom lens and bring that to bear on the detail within your selected area. Now you are aware of a multiplicity of details which were simply not available to you before. We suggest that the zoom-lens effect is produced by the use of language in the context of situation. It makes some particular details highly salient and draws attention to them. The language used brings into play in the mind of the listeners resonances of previous, similar, experiences (consider the 'mine-for-yours' swapping of experiences which we illustrated in chapter 2, extracts (2.11)–(2.14)). It also permits him to build a model in his mind from what the speaker is saying, a model which the listener may enrich with experiences far beyond those intended by the speaker. The effect of this interaction of the limiting effect of context on the speaker's global experience and the expanding effect of the speech event within that context is illustrated in figure 3.3. This expanding effect is vividly described by Bartlett, one of the founding fathers of modern psychology:

> It is legitimate to say that all cognitive processes which have been considered . . . are ways in which some fundamental 'effort after meaning' seeks expression. Speaking very broadly, such effort is simply the attempt *to connect something that is given with something other than itself.* (1932; our emphasis)

The listener will attempt to relate what he hears to his own relevant experience thus bringing into play the relevant detail of his own experience. Comprehension is not simply 'the reduction of uncertainty', as has sometimes been claimed; it is also 'the integration into experience'. If this is a correct outline of what we mean by 'comprehension', then one thing that should be extremely clear is that it is a process that we could not possibly pretend to *teach*.

Given that students need to learn to interpret utterances spoken in their target language, what is the teacher able to offer them? It seems that he should be able to offer all the facilitating devices and strategies at his disposal, which will put the student in the most advantageous position to learn for himself how to understand what is said by people, with intentions to communicate, in the foreign language.

3.4 Native listening: strategies

The native listener normally experiences spoken language in a situational context where he is aware of 'significant' features of context even before anyone speaks at all. Sometimes, however, even the native listener experiences spoken language which is relatively 'out of context'. How does he behave then? If you observe the behaviour of someone coming up and joining a group of other people who are already engaged in a conversation, you will notice that the new arrival usually waits for a minute or two before beginning to take part in the conversation, to give himself time to work out what is being talked about and what sort of attitudes are being expressed by different participants. The tactful individual joins in the conversation rather carefully and, even so, may sometimes find that he has guessed wrong and that the participants are in fact talking about something other than what he has worked out they must be talking about. Even native listeners then may occasionally find it difficult to work out the precise topic, purposes and attitudes of largely interactional conversations, even given that they have a lot of information about the context of situation. The native listener will give himself *time* to work out what is going on, and will frequently have to work quite hard, making very active use of the limiting constraints of his previous experience.

The position is rather similar when he turns on the radio or television. He has to use all the incoming cues, in a highly active manner, to determine who is speaking and why, to whom, and in what situation. In this case he is working out what the context must be from the language. He can only do this in the light of his previous experience of similar texts. If he tunes in to a radio programme where an elderly man is talking about the effects of rain on the harvest, a whole range of possible programmes may be at issue: a programme illustrating rural dialects, an agricultural programme for farmers, a news broadcast with one illustrative farmer expressing gloom, an advertisement for water sprinklers, a documentary programme about rural life in south-west England, etc. A very wide range (opening up) of possible situations can be constructed on the basis of the listener's experience of previous texts uttered in contexts. Note, though, that all the possibilities must comfortably include an elderly man talking about the effects of rain on harvest (narrowing down), i.e. not be discussions between atomic physicists, or news broadcasts on the Italian fashion industry, or a programme on cordon bleu cooking. If the listener continues listening and, when the elderly man stops speaking, he hears a woman replying in rather similar terms, who then goes on to mention the matrimonial activities of one of their children, he will probably assume, on the basis of this further evidence, that the programme is nothing to do with any of the programme types we have listed above, but is a radio play of some sort, perhaps 'an every day story of country folk'. Progressively, as the listener listens, he will narrow down his assessment of the *type*, in global terms, of discourse that he is listening to and which he is succeeding in constructing a mental context for. Simultaneously, he will be enriching, on the basis of his previous experience, the model he is constructing in his mind of what *actually* is going on.

On the basis of his previous experience of discourse, the native listener will identify a discourse as containing one type of language rather than another. He will recognise the difference between largely interactional language, where what is primarily at issue is people being nice to each other, and primarily transactional language, where what is at issue is the transfer of information. He will recognise the difference between language which is directly addressed to him and intended as an instruction, and language which, like a news broadcast, is intended to inform him about what the world is like. He will attribute different purposes in speaking to speakers. He will not suppose that speakers always, or even mostly, speak in order to inform. He will assume that the occasion of speaking is frequently used for the transmission of attitude – that the speaker is cross about something, or mystified, or that he is being kind or condescending or aggressive or polite.

The native listener will assume that speakers will package what they want to say in a way that is appropriate to their listeners. The speaker will generally conform to the philosopher Grice's maxims of co-operative conversation, which we can represent thus:

1 Quality – say only what you know to be true.
2 Quantity – say as much as your listener needs in order to understand, but don't tell him what he knows already.
3 Relevance – make what you say relevant to the purposes of the conversation.
4 Manner – say what you need to say clearly and unambiguously.

We have to assume, in the general run of life, that speakers are telling the truth. Telling a lie is an aberration, and society will tend to stamp it out, because it is necessary for society to organise itself as far as possible on the expectation of truth and trust. When speakers say things they are not sure about, they can mark the insecure status of what they are saying with modal phrases like: *I think, perhaps, we might assume, it seems likely, it's possible, I should like to believe*, etc. The listener will assume that the speaker is telling him the truth, or that the speaker will mark what he is not sure about. The listener may repeat the content to some future listener in a number of ways. He may say:

(3.6)   (a) X is the case
             (b) B told me that X is the case
             (c) B told me that he thinks that X is the case

(3.6c) may strictly report the detail of what happened. (3.6a) and (3.6b) may represent what our listener believes B meant. Only the most pedantic person would always in all circumstances report the whole of (c). An important *caveat* to Grice's maxim of 'quality' must be that we should expect that speakers will tell the truth, *as they perceive it*. Native speakers, over time, become used to dealing with this modified view of truth. They do not expect 100 per cent 'truth', a God-like vision.

Listeners expect speakers to package what they say so that the listener can understand it. The speaker has to consider the 'information gap' which exists between him and his listener. He has to decide how much information he needs to make explicit to his listener, so that the listener can thoroughly understand what is being said. It will be boring for the listener if the speaker, as some speakers do, recapitulates the history of the world, before telling him that rooks nest at the tops of trees (quantity). It will equally be boring and pointless for the listener if the speaker tells him something and he is not at all sure what the something is that he is being told about (manner). The speaker has a delicate line to tread here. It is a noticeable feature of conversations that speakers often use questions to test out their listener's state of knowledge on a particular topic:

(3.7)   A: they're going to pay the children to stay at school + did
               you hear about that?
           B: no + really +
           A: uh hm + that's the news today + mine'll be going back
               + they've to be paid seven pounds a week in Sheffield
               + it's a trial thing

(3.8)   A: there were more slums (in Glasgow) + what used to be
               the Gorbals + you'd pass through there (oh) + + they
               talk about a miracle and it is a miracle + + if you could
               just picture what it was + there're big high flats – did
               you pass through there?
           B: yes + uh huh
           A: that's the Gorbals

(3.9)   A: where I stayed was in Mea + was off Morningside
               Road + +
           B: oh + yes + that's not far from where Grandpa's house
               +
           A: yes + just further on + in the bus + you know the
               Plaza + there was a Plaza + do you remember it +
               further on
           B: erm +
           A: it was the next stop
           B: oh yes + it's now something else

In (3.7) A asks B whether she knows about 'paying the children to
stay at school' and, having checked that she does not, goes on to tell
her about it. In (3.8) A checks that B knows the place she is referring
to before going on to talk about recent changes there. In (3.9) A is
particularly concerned to get the location right, and, dissatisfied with
B's wary reply *erm*, continues to add detail until B identifies the place
where 'the Plaza' used to be. This checking of the listener's state of
knowledge is a normal procedure in conversation (except of course
in conversations between student and teacher, where it is often
very hard for the student to judge the teacher's actual or pretended
state of ignorance since, conventionally, the teacher takes a very
knowledgeable role).

Grice's third maxim, the maxim of 'relevance', of course relates
back to the interpretive strategy we summarised in the principle
of analogy. The speaker continues to talk on the same topic,
maintaining the same place and time up to the moment when he gives
explicit notice of a change in one of these features.

The native listener expects the principles of truth and trust
embodied in Grice's maxims to operate over what the speaker says
and how he says it. This expectation gives him the confidence to
interpret what is not clear in the message or what doesn't make sense

in terms of the coherent model of what is being said that he is constructing in his mind. If he hears a snippet like that represented in extract (3.1) as [kɑ̣trɪmwɒt] he will confidently interpret that in context as meaning 'I can't remember what (they are)'. Gross phonetic simplification constantly occurs in speech, but the native listener does not even notice it. He merely samples the incoming message, particularly the stressed peaks which tend to be articulated more clearly, and constructs an interpretation on the basis of his sampling and on how well the interpretation fits in with (is coherent with) the mental model he is busy constructing.

Similarly, if the native listener fails to hear part of the message because a bus goes by, or the speaker turns his head away, or some other person coughs, he does not abandon the construction of his model. Occasionally, he may miss something vital and not be able to reconstruct an adequate interpretation. At this point, if it's possible, he will stop the speaker and ask him to repeat what he has said. If it is a question of having understood the words spoken, but not having understood what the speaker could possibly *mean* by what he has said, the native listener may demand clarification, or justification, or some detail of background knowledge which he happens not to have, but which the speaker has assumed he had.

The native listener will not normally expect to remember everything that he hears. He will select from what he hears that which seems to him crucial for him to develop a coherent mental model. A good deal of detail will not be recorded in a form which he will remember. It is very rare, unless some striking phrase has been used, for a listener to remember the verbal detail of what was said for long after it was uttered. (Just think for a moment what a monumental memory load would be involved if such a process actually took place.) What principles determine what, of something that is said, the listener puts saliently into his mental model and is likely to remember?

First, the listener's own personal interests will be a powerful determiner of what he abstracts from what is said. In addition, the strategy he adopts will, in part, be determined by the purpose that he attributes to the speaker in speaking. If he thinks the speaker intends to give him detailed instructions, all of which he has to remember, the listener will expect to be addressed in very short bursts (thirty seconds to a minute), not to be expected to remember more than five elements or so, and, moreover, he will expect the speaker to repeat what he has said, possibly several times. If there are more than five pieces of detail which the listener has to remember, and they are not already well known to him, he will probably need to write down a note of them. If the listener attributes quite a different intention to his speaker, for instance, that he is telling him a funny anecdote, he will construct a mental model of the main participants and events and keep on scanning the input with respect to those participants and events to see if he can discern what is funny. We have to assume that listeners adopt different strategies of interpretation for different types of discourse.

Consider again the situation of the foreign learner in the typical listening comprehension lesson. He is usually asked to listen to a fairly long (three minutes or more) chunk of speech which is never addressed to him, but where he is always in the position of overhearer. As an overhearer he has to reconstruct from the language, which he only partially understands, the context of situation in which this language would make sense. From the language which he only partially understands in this reconstructed context, he needs to be able to determine intentions for speakers, in order to know what the appropriate processing strategy is. Moreover, he knows that, at the end of the listening, he will be confronted by a set of questions which ask him precisely what was said, at regular intervals of time; these questions will frequently ignore the purpose of the speaker in speaking, they will totally undervalue his own native experience of language, and assume a notion of 100 per cent correctness in interpretation. It is hardly surprising that, despite the enormous amount of energy going into the production of listening materials, foreign learners who have gone through listening comprehension courses still find immense problems with understanding the spoken form of the foreign language when it is addressed to them.

Surely we can offer the student better opportunities of learning to listen as a native listener does.

3.5 Background: British background and culture

We shall talk in this section as though we were exclusively concerned with teaching British English. It should be apparent that on all occasions 'American English' (or 'French' or 'Italian') could be substituted.

Many courses for teaching a foreign language include a component which has a name like 'Background and culture'. Sometimes these components are seen mainly as the background to the literature component of the course, to give an account of the society in which, for instance, a novel is set. Sometimes these components are seen mainly as contributing the background knowledge of society which will enable foreign learners to talk or write or read about the sorts of things that people in that society know. Both of these aims seem perfectly reasonable. What is surprising, however, is the level at which these components are often set. The level usually appears to derive from a mixture of a potted 'British history and institutions' course, often combined with a few extracts which might relate to 'a tourist's guide to London'. Certainly, information about Britain which might be relevant to the student one day is imparted in such courses. Much of the detail of the information is informative, sometimes surprising, to the *native* reader. 'Goodness me!' you exclaim to yourself as you read, 'I didn't know that'. That phenomenon should surely strike us as odd, if the aim of the component is to impart that knowledge of British background and culture *which British native speakers* are generally assumed to know.

A more modest approach than one which attempts to distinguish and describe the main features of British institutions might usefully be added to this major undertaking. The modest approach would specifically use the British background and culture course, on occasions when this is appropriate, to provide the sorts of cultural stereotypes which British speakers assume their listeners share with them, and which British listeners assume in interpretation. Such an approach would demand an analysis of the language to be experienced in terms of the features of context which we described in section 3.4. The language to be experienced would of course be that which is to be encountered in the next written comprehension or listening comprehension lesson. The aim of the component would be to consider types of speakers, types of listeners, types of place / time, situations of context, which rouse different expectations in the native listener. To consider also types of genre (fairy stories, anecdotes etc.) and the part they play in a culture – to draw attention to the sort of 'hero' which a particular culture establishes ('little man makes good' as in David and Goliath, and innumerable stories where the poor farmer's third son marries the princess, and Charlie Chaplin; 'super physical-man' as in Hercules, Tarzan, James Bond, Superman himself, cowboys, pilots and football heroes; the 'get-up-and-go man' – more popular in America than Britain – Al Capone, 'JR' in *Dallas*, etc.). To consider what is culturally deemed 'success' or 'failure' or 'just desserts'. The *point* of most narratives or anecdotes is not simply to *inform* the listener , as we keep repeating, but to draw a moral, to justify a position, to exemplify a point. All of these imply *value-judgments* of one sort or another, and value-judgments are precisely what differ from one culture to the next, and even within different sectors of the same culture. If the student is to understand the language he is exposed to, 'understanding' must imply 'seeing the point' of the language. The student must have enough background knowledge of the culture, knowledge which is relevant to the particular instance of the language he is concerned with, to enable him to assess why what is being said is being said. It is clearly the case that in cultures closest to British culture, cultural values will, in many cases, overlap. It is extremely unlikely that they will overlap totally. What was intended by the speaker who asserted that Sir Harold Wilson, when prime minister, 'liked HP sauce'? Which sections of society would even think of making such an assertion? What is intended by asserting that Mr Roy Jenkins, as leader of a political alliance party, 'likes claret'? Which sections of society would make that assertion? Would those two assertions be made by the same people?

The more distant the culture, in terms of values and expectations, the more important it is that students be prepared, in 'background' classes, to understand what it is that people who are producing the target language care about, notice, bother to talk about, make judgments about. It is not sufficient for the student to be told that the British talk about 'the weather', whereas the French talk about 'food'. Such assertions may be true, but they are only the beginning of the socio-cultural exploration which will enable the foreign learner to appreciate why members of a particular society talk at all.

Background: the speaker's voice

A resource which is commonly overlooked in listening comprehension courses is the voice of the speaker. It is usually possible to tell, from the voice alone, the sex of the speaker and also the age, within rather wide ranges. Most people can distinguish a child's voice from that of an adolescent, an adolescent voice from that of a speaker in his early twenties, the voice of a young speaker from that of a middle-aged speaker, a middle-aged voice from that of an elderly or extremely old speaker. In making such identifications we are of course relying on experience, on stereotypes. It is also possible for another native speaker of a language to identify the probable level of education of a speaker, and, often, to identify from his accent (pronunciation), whereabouts he comes from. Social information of this sort, which is normally of course quite unintended by the speaker, since it constitutes *who* he is, will often guide the listener to interpret what the speaker says in terms of expectations raised by the appropriate stereotypes. It will immediately be obvious that there is a danger in stereotypes, since a particular individual may have developed a particularly prejudiced view of people who share a stereotypical feature, from some previous prejudicial experience of his own or of his community. Racial prejudice immediately comes to mind, class prejudice, educational, political, and religious prejudice. It would be absurd to pretend that the dangers of prejudice arising from false or misleading interpretation of stereotypes does not exist. Clearly it does. However, to let the misuse of stereotypical classification blind us to the fact that we organise our lives in terms of such a principle, that all interpretation is primarily based on analogy with a classified past experience, would obviously be equally absurd. Where stereotypes are damaging, we must hope that they will be modified, but like the Editors of the *Oxford English Dictionary*, if we are interested in how people interpret language, it is our job to record relevant factors. We rely on stereotypes in our interpretation of what is said to us in terms of whether it sounds authoritative / pompous / complacent/ condescending / hesitant / biassed / ignorant. We rely on them, but riskily, because our expectations often have to be modified (which is how, we assume, the stereotypes get modified). A former student who spoke with a rich provincial accent remarked of an RP speaker who spoke particularly 'plummily' that, for two terms, he had supposed this RP student 'wasn't really human', but had discovered, to his surprise, in their third term, that the student was really 'actually nice, quite human', just 'couldn't help speaking like that'. A stereotype fortunately modified.

We can deduce more than sex, age, level of education, and place of origin, by listening to the speaker's voice. Listeners often have expectations of the size, and physical characteristics, of people whose voices they hear only on the radio or telephone or tape. Sometimes listeners judge that a speaker is unwell – feels 'weak' or 'nervy' or has a cold. It's possible to make local judgments on the speaker's physical situation like 'is speaking with his mouth full' or 'is drunk'. It is possible also to make personality judgments like 'is confident / shy / extrovert / optimistic' on the basis of experience of the speaker's voice. It is not clear how far judgments of this kind can be made cross-culturally. Certainly people seem prepared to make such judgments about the personalities of speakers speaking a language which the listeners do not understand, that is, on the basis of the speaker's voice alone, with no indication of the verbal message. On the basis of anecdotal experience of British speakers reacting to native speakers of Greek, for example, it seems possible that personality stereotypes are not completely interchangeable from one culture to another. If it should be shown that cross-cultural misunderstandings do arise from the application of inappropriate stereotypes to judgments of personality based on speakers' voices, a valuable part of a listening comprehension course would include comment on the *native* stereotype attached to a particular type of speaker's voice. (The study of actors' adoption of different voice qualities to play different stereotypical roles would be of interest here.)

Listeners make judgments not only about the personality which they attribute to a particular speaker's voice, but also about the role which particular speakers are playing and the attitude they are expressing. Most of the data illustrated on our tape is produced by speakers who are speaking in a cheerful friendly voice – the norm for most adult working relationships. How do we tell if a speaker is being friendly? Consider extract (3.10) which is part of a longer extract on the tape.

(3.10) (9)   A: could you describe how you got from your home to the
                  school + if you remember (breathy giggle)
             B: the exact route (road?)
             A: if you remember it (high in pitch range, creaky – slight
                  giggle)
             B;   good grief │ (breathy voice, long syllables) │ what a funny
                            │ A: (vaguely?)   │
                  question – ye-ah + yes I can (long syllables, 'warm
                  voice quality', big intonation movements in the higher
                  part of his pitch range) │ erm + perfectly   │
                                           │ A: (breathy giggles)   │

B in particular manifests a 'warm' voice quality, not under any nervous strain, taking his time, with long syllables and lots of intonational movement. A produces supportive breathy giggles (note also her supportive friendly noises in the rest of this extract, transcribed and discussed in section 3.7). Observe, incidentally, that you were able to recognise the sex of each speaker. You probably have a reasonable idea of their ages (not seven or seventy), some idea of where they come from and their level of education (both educated Scottish speakers). If you heard this extract on the radio as you entered a room, even before you were able to identify any words being spoken, you would almost certainly be able to identify the genre, the sort of talk that is going on, the fact that this is a non-stressful friendly conversation. The voices alone indicate this – the speakers are taking their time, partially overlapping, giggling, speaking with no indication of nervous tension. Listening to the tape without listening to the words, simply identifying the genre, provides valuable background information.

Consider another example, extract (3.11), also on the tape. Listen to this and decide what sort of person the speaker is and what sort of role is being adopted by the speaker, hence what sort of genre we're likely to be concerned with here.

(3.11) (4)   A: now there + are + vulnerable + people + around +
and it is + erm + it's part of a + humane society + that
it sets out + sometimes at some inconvenience to the
mass of the population + to protect + the vulnerable
people + + and + + I think it's very much worth doing

Presumably you have decided that the speaker is a man, middle-aged,
highly educated, an RP speaker. Without listening to the content of
what he is saying, you have almost certainly determined that he is *not*
having an intimate private conversation with a single listener. He is
obviously speaking quite loudly, slowly, deliberately, thinking about
what he is saying as he says it – hence the frequent pausing – but used
to speaking in public in this way – hence the easy, unflustered rhythm
which incorporates the pausing. He is obviously a practised public
speaker, speaking in public. Recognition of this genre will lead the
listener *not* to expect the sort of content that he associates with
exchanges between people waiting at a bus-stop or talking to a shop
assistant.

In the next short extract, there are two main speakers, both
professional men, RP-speaking academics in their thirties. They are
discussing the distribution of the unstressed vowels [ɪ] and [ə] in
words like *basket* and *system*, a professional discussion.

(3.12) (5)   A: well in my case + the incidence of [ɪ] + well he decided
it was an Americanism + w-what he based that on I
don't know
    B: as in what sort of words
    A: well I mean + city + +
    B: city + +
    A: erm + + but that I I I don't(?) shown (?) I mean this
would would be straight Daniel Jones
    B: wh+wh+wh+what would you be supposed to
       say| + | instead of city
          |C: yes|

A has just quoted an opinion on his speech which was voiced by an
eminent authority. B then asks a direct, rather flat, question which
requests examples of the sort of word involved. A provides one quite
quickly, *city*. B repeats this word, low in his voice range, slowly
('reflectively') – *city*. A, who speaks throughout in what we might
characterise as a 'nervous' manner, in short rapid bursts with a good
deal of stuttering, now launches into a prolonged stutter as he
realises that the word he has provided does not exemplify the point at
issue. B now asks a second question, which he produces in a manner
very different from the first one. He produces a 'sympathetic'
stuttered onset to *what*, and then an elaborate modal structure *would*

you be supposed to say, and goes high into his pitch range on *city*. Whereas his first question was a very straightforward request for examples, his second question is produced with a good deal more elaboration, presumably because he has inadvertently put speaker A into a difficult position which A now has to get out of. We have already quoted Sacks' procedural question 'why this, to me, now' which listeners need to consider in constructing an interpretation of what is addressed to them. We need to add to this a further procedural question 'why like this' in order to take account of the 'it's not so much what he said but the way he said it' phenomenon.

As native listeners we react to the way a speaker says something at a level far below consciousness, much of the time. In order to think about the effect *the way* something is spoken has on our interpretation of what is said, we need to bring to a conscious level variability in the voice of the speaker. The way the speaker speaks provides information about the identity of the speaker, his personality, his attitude, and the type of genre he is participating in. None of this will help the listener to predict precisely what will be uttered. All of this should, however, combine to limit the listener's expectation of what is likely to be said, on the one hand, and, on the other, should be available to modify his interpretation of what is actually said, simply because it is said by a person of such-and-such a sort, on such-and-such an occasion, speaking more or less confidently, or in a more or less authoritative manner.

3.6 Choosing materials

Obviously the sort of material which is selected for a particular course will be selected on criteria which are determined by the aims of the course. If the course is primarily intended to enable students to adopt the role of tourists in the foreign country, then they should be exposed to language used in short interactional turns and in short transactional turns. If the course is primarily intended to enable students to follow lectures in the foreign language, then they have to work towards coping with long transactional turns, and will certainly need a note-taking component. We shall assume a general intermediate course level here, but the principles we shall discuss apply equally to other levels.

Grading materials: by speaker

There is no doubt that it is easier to understand a tape when only one person is speaking. This gives an opportunity to get used to that particular individual's habits of speech and, particularly, his characteristic rhythm and pause structures. It is clearly helpful if the speaker is, to begin with, one who characteristically speaks slowly. Speakers who speak slowly, characteristically speak relatively clearly. Our stereotypical slow speaker would be a large, elderly, rather pompous man.

It is important that the speaker does not adopt a style of speech we characterised earlier as that spoken to the foreigner, the stupid or the deaf. As soon as people begin to slow their speech down artificially, they tend to adopt habits of articulation and rhythmic structure which are quite uncharacteristic of normal speech. Students trained on speech of this type are trained to listen to a style of speech they will seldom, if ever, hear again. That is why it is important to find a naturally slow speaker and, where possible, one who does not know that he is addressing a foreign student.

In the early stages of a course all the taped speakers should speak a rather similar type of accent. If British English is the aim, then 'demotic' RP, the educated speech of those who live in the south of England, should probably be the model. It is important, however, since these speakers will contribute to the model of spoken English produced by the foreign learner, that they should not generally be speakers of 'advanced RP', that peculiarly 'plummy-voiced' and rather loudly-articulated version of RP which is associated in the minds of the rest of the population with excessive complacency and expectation of privilege (social facts which are relevant to understanding, for instance, why Mr Roy Jenkins is characterised as 'liking claret').

As the course progresses, the student may be exposed to tapes with more than one speaker, preferably, to begin with, of different sexes since this should enable him to distinguish easily between the speakers. The student will then, necessarily, adopt the role of 'overhearer'. It is quite difficult even for practised native speakers to follow a conversation on tape with four or more participants; three is probably the most you can handle comfortably. Note that professional broadcasts always identify speakers clearly and ration the length of their turns when more than three speakers participate in a 'discussion' or conversation.

As the students progress, speakers of other accents may be introduced, though 'extreme' accents should probably be avoided even with advanced students, since even native speakers often find considerable difficulty with an accent which is very different from the ones they are most accustomed to hearing or speaking.

Grading materials: by intended listener

Most materials currently on the market consist of recordings of individuals giving lectures / speeches, etc. or of dialogues between two individuals, in some cases 'natural', in some cases 'read aloud'.

The problem with formal speech / lecture material is that it is often difficult in content, and that it is not clear how to use such extended turns in listening practice so as not to put an unreasonable demand on the foreign learner in the early stages. We shall return to this problem in the next section.

The problem with the dialogues is a) that they turn the listener into an overhearer, and b) how to make their content in any way interesting. It is possible to write zippy and amusing dialogues which can then be read aloud. There is no reason at all why such input should not occasionally form part of the foreign learner's diet. It prepares him to listen to radio / TV / film dialogue or indeed, in general, to listen to theatrical dialogue. We have already pointed out, however, that it does not prepare the student to listen to normal spontaneous spoken language. It consists of written language read aloud. It will tend to consist of complete sentences, pausing at the end of sentences, well-worked-out language, relatively well-packed with information. It may bear rather little resemblance, except for the fact that it is spoken, to spontaneous speech. It cannot therefore offer a substitute for training with real spontaneous speech. Let us reiterate that there is no reason for not using written dialogue read aloud sometimes. After all, many a native listener listens to the radio programme 'A book at bed-time' before retiring each night!

If the zealous course-constructor decides to opt for spontaneous conversation, more or less surreptitiously recorded, he immediately meets a further problem. Most conversations are appallingly boring. It is the *participation* in conversations which makes us such avid talkers, the 'need to know' or 'the need to tell' or 'the need to be friendly'. You can listen to hours and hours of recorded conversation without finding anything that interests you from the point of view of what the speakers are talking about or what they are saying about it. After all, their conversation was not intended for the overhearer. It was intended for them as participants. This is often hard for course-constructors to realise because, after a while, anyone who listens to a lot of recorded conversation turns into a conversation analyst and begins to use his analytic observation. Once this happens, any fragment of conversation, however intrinsically boring as to topic, becomes fascinating from the point of view of the interaction, how who says what, how who is friendly to whom, how who ever-so-discreetly disagrees, how who plays for time, and so on. It seems likely that if foreign learners are to find any interest in what are really often extremely dull conversations, they have to be provided with tasks which help them to become, in however limited a way, conversation analysts too.

Clearly there must exist conversations which would be interesting to some students. Many a course-constructor would like to have a recording of what the man who broke into the Queen's bedroom discussed with her. There is widespread interest in the Watergate tapes. Tapes illustrating police corruption, the interrogation of spies, the 'breaking' of members of the Mafia, all have a certain ghastly fascination. The sociolinguist Labov found that people were always very ready to talk about 'danger of death'. It may be that those tapes would be interesting to listen to, though we suspect that 'danger of *my* death' would be intrinsically more interesting than 'danger of *his* death'. The perennially interesting conversations presumably are concerned with power, sex and danger (real in all cases). It is hardly conceivable to suppose that it would be possible to construct a listening comprehension course based only on such topics. The constant problem for the teacher, though, is usually presented as 'finding interesting material'.

It seems to us likely that it is, in principle, not possible to find material which would interest everyone. It follows that the emphasis should be moved from attempting to provide intrinsically interesting materials, which we have just claimed is generally impossible, to *doing interesting things* with materials which may be boring but may, from time to time, strike a chord with some student; these materials should be chosen, not so much on the basis of their own interest, as for what they can be used to do. 'Doing interesting things' is probably a stronger claim than anything we can suggest would justify. What we mean by this, basically, is doing a much wider variety of things in the listening comprehension class, and actively involving the listener in reacting to language rather than simply 'answering questions' on what he has overheard. We shall return to this topic in section 3.7.

Grading materials: by content

Surprisingly little is known about what constitutes more or less 'difficult' content. Much of the work done on 'readability' is concerned with more or less complex syntactic structures. We have already suggested that complex syntax is rarely found in spoken language until you get to the level of listening to university lectures or political speeches (language much influenced by written language). Simple measures of syntactic complexity are unlikely to get us very

far in assessing the difficulty of understanding different chunks of
spoken language.

Advanced, specialised, vocabulary may provide a source of
difficulty if it is unfamiliar, and it is probably reasonably sound
pedagogic practice to ensure that students have already encountered
crucial terminology, glossed in the sense it has in the passage, before
they encounter a chunk of language. It seems at least possible,
however, that some of the difficulty in understanding spoken
language arises not so much from the use of highly specialised
vocabulary, but from the very generalised use of very general
vocabulary. Consider the following extract from a conversation:

(3.13)   A: the system they have over there is that they study at
                      university + and then work in the summer + for a firm
                      + and the firm that Joe first worked for + were
                      desperate to have him back +

                B: oh + were they really + +

                A: the next year and the next year + and + 'we'll give you
                      a job as soon as you come out' +

                B: is that so + they do that quite a bit here + my
                      girlfriend's son – he's got his BSc at Glasgow University
                      but he was employed + by Barr and Strouds (coughs)
                      + + and he was testing erm + periscope lenses + I
                      think he was failing more than he was passing (laughs)
                      + + they + the Navy have a very high standard for
                      such things and er his + Neil's standards are equally
                      high

There may well be 'hard' vocabulary which needs to be glossed:
university, firm, BSc, Barr and Strouds (the student's guess may be as
good as ours here), *periscope lenses, the Navy, standard* for example.
It seems, though, at least plausible that expressions which do not
contain 'hard vocabulary' but, rather, very general vocabulary, may
be difficult to interpret like: *the system they have over there, is that
they study, were desperate to have him back, were they really, the
next year and the next year, we'll give you a job, they do that quite a
bit here, such things, equally high*. It is often not being sure who or
what expressions like *they, him, we'll, you, that, here, such things*
refer to, which constitutes the problem for the student. Moreover,
it may not be what is actually *expressed* in the text at all which
constitutes the difficulty for the student, but the amount of background knowledge which is assumed to be shared or inferrable.
We would assume that the more the background knowledge which is
assumed in a particular discourse, the more difficult that discourse
will be for the student to understand if he does not share that
knowledge.

If this assumption is correct, it follows that what ought to be easiest for the student to understand must be content which he is most familiar with, either in virtue of his own similar cultural experience, or in view of his own areas of expertise, or in virtue of having been thoroughly prepared for the type of discourse he is to listen to.

It seems likely that the genres which are relatively easy to listen to are those same genres which are relatively easy to produce. We would predict, on this basis, that narratives and instructions would be easier to understand than abstract argument, explanation or justification.

If the patterns of difficulty of comprehension follow the patterns of difficulty in production, then we will expect that narratives with few participants and a rather straightforward temporal structure will be easier to understand than narratives with more participants (especially same-gender participants) and more complex temporal structure. We shall expect that instructions or descriptions involving fewer entities, with a few simple relationships, will be easier to understand than ones which involve more entities and more, more complex, relationships.

Following on this argument (all of which needs to be carefully scrutinised), we shall assume that discourse which maximally involves the listener will be more comprehensible than discourse which does not involve the listener. One obvious reason for this is that the listener constitutes part of the context and if that part of the context, at least, is known to him, he controls some part of the relevant knowledge of context. How could the listener be maximally involved? One solution may be, sometimes, to use taped material which addresses the listener directly and gives him instructions on how to fulfil a particular task (a task involving assembling, drawing, visual discrimination, paper-folding, numerical computation, or whatever). Setting a task of a suitable level of difficulty for the cognitive level of the student is probably more taxing on the imagination than finding the relevant level of difficulty in the language.

Grading materials: by support

We assume that the more external support is offered to a listener, the easier it is for him to understand the language used. Most people find it very much easier to understand the foreign language which they see produced in a dramatic context on a film, than when it is simply played on tape. The visual environment gives an enormously important extra dimension of information. Not only does it permit the listener to see what the participants look like, whether they are young or old, rich or poor, indoors or out of doors, together with all the details of the features of the physical context, it also permits him to see the physical relationships between the participants, how close they stand or sit to each other, whether or not they touch each other, whether they lean towards each other in a friendly fashion as they speak, or whether they turn away from each other. With the explosion of video technology, we must hope that fewer and fewer students, in the early stages of a listening comprehension course, will encounter the foreign spoken language without the support of the visual environment.

Even when advanced students are practising listening to lectures in a foreign language, it is important to realise that a video tape is still an immense help. It might seem that to have an extensive video tape of one man talking in front of a blackboard would be a waste of the video facility. On the contrary. To begin with, it is helpful for the student to develop a visual stereotype to interpenetrate with his auditory stereotype of what a lecture means. Then it is helpful for most listeners, whether foreigners or not, to watch the face of the person who is speaking, for at least some of the time. It is quite helpful to be able to observe the movements of the speaker's lips and jaw, at least initially, since they give an indication of the utterance of labial consonants, open vowels, rounded consonants and vowels, which reinforces the auditory input. It is quite helpful, too, to be able to observe the extra articulatory effort on a stressed syllable (in a stress language like English) which often coincides with larger facial gestures like raising and lowering the eyebrows, as well as with nodding or shaking the head (most speakers constantly move their heads as they speak) and with gestures of the hands, shoulders, etc. These larger gestures are often employed by a speaker to emphasise a particularly important point – and such gestures should certainly serve as a cue to students that this is a point they should pay attention to. Quite apart from all this extra information about what he is saying, a lecturer in front of a blackboard will often write points up on the blackboard, and it is particularly helpful for the foreign student to learn what sort of points get written up, how different lecturers use blackboards, how to spell technical terms, etc.

A further obvious support, which needs careful handling, is a transcript of the spoken text. Where the student has had a good deal of experience with the written language or feels more secure with the written language than with the spoken language, it seems perfectly reasonable, from time to time, particularly with introductory portions of longer texts, to provide a written transcript. It is important that the written transcript should be presented as the

transcript of the spoken language and not tidied up to look like
written language, since it will hardly be helpful to the student if he
keeps finding gross mismatches between what he thinks he hears and
what is represented on the page. So pauses and *ums* and *erms*, laughs
and coughs should be indicated, and incomplete utterances left
uncompleted. Where it is not quite clear what the speaker said,
the transcriber should mark this unclarity in the transcription, to
reassure the hearer that he can't be expected to hear everything, and
to make it clear that, if this is an important bit of the message which
has got obscured, the listener will have to do some interpretive work
to determine what was *likely* to have been said. Often, of course, the
bits that are unclear are not crucial to the message anyway, and it is
positively valuable for the listener to be reassured that he does not
need to hear everything all the time in order to arrive at a reasonable
interpretation. Where the teacher is using the tape to draw attention
to characteristic features of taking up a turn, for example, it is
positively valuable for the student to be able to study these, both in
the transcribed version, and on tape.

It is not hard to imagine other types of support for the language –
photographs, maps, cartoons, scientific diagrams, graphs, etc. It is
essential, of course, that the student should be thoroughly familiar
with the nature of the support. It would be absurd to use a set of
graphs to support language which was discussing variation in
population growth, if the listener was not extremely competent in
reading information from graphs.

In the early stages of any course, in order to ensure that the student
experiences *success* in arriving at a reasonable interpretation of the
foreign language, as many helpful support systems as possible should
be provided. As the student progresses, reliance on external support
can gradually be withdrawn. This in itself will indicate the student's
progress, in relying less and less on external supports, and more
and more on language. The teacher should not forget, however,
that really difficult, complex, material, like a radio version of a
Shakespeare play, is something that most native speakers would
prefer to listen to with a written text before them, and that many
native speakers spend a large part of their lives watching television.
When a point arrives in a course when a distinction can be drawn
between close analytic listening that students do with the teacher in
class, and the extended listening for pleasure (and for establishing
a wide range of stereotypes from increasing experience of the
language), it may be that video and transcript supports should be
mostly used for supporting the extended listening which the student
does alone.

Choosing materials: types of purpose

The standard format for listening comprehension teaching is for a course to consist of varied dialogues and monologues chosen as far as possible, and often very imaginatively, for their 'intrinsic interest', which tend to run for a roughly equal length of time. A typical class consists of the teacher playing the tape, and the students answering questions on the tape. As we have already remarked, the questions tend to be fairly equally distributed throughout the written transcript of the text, and in general deal with 'facts', information that has been specifically stated in the text or which can be directly inferred from the text.

If the intention of a course is that students should be exposed to more than one type of text, then different texts need to be chosen on the basis not only of variation in *topic*, which seems to have been the main criterion so far in most courses, but in terms of the *purposes* for which the text was intended. If a text was produced by two speakers who were simply 'being friendly' and taking short interactional turns, then that short text should be studied as an example of that genre. Students should not be asked to answer questions concerning the 'facts' communicated in such a discourse. The 'facts' are more or less irrelevant to the purpose of the discourse. They should pay attention to what the discourse was produced for, and observe the various strategies of being friendly that the participants manifest. This demands an analytic, careful, consideration which not all students may be prepared to produce. If the students prefer working with tapes which provide 'facts', then it is clearly more appropriate for them to work with transactional turns where the *point* of the communication is the transfer of information.

One basis for selection of texts is that they should be chosen to illustrate the different things that language is used for in real life, and presented in a manner which relates as far as possible to the way that sort of purpose is dealt with in language in real life. Thus an instructional text containing detailed information should either be very short and repeated, in the way a person giving route directions to a tourist will repeat what he said, several times over sometimes, or it should be produced by a speaker who is actually giving instructions to another student who does the task as he listens. That is to say, the language will be produced at a speed, and with the appropriate pausing, to permit the instructions to be followed. It is not adequate to ask a speaker giving instructions to 'imagine' that he is speaking to someone who is carrying out those instructions. We have found that such speakers produce far less information, and produce it more rapidly, than speakers who are talking to genuine performing listeners.

If the discourse consists of a discussion which slides between one person seriously informing another and the second person commenting on this, and the student is obliged to adopt the role of overhearer, the tape may be used for two quite distinct purposes (to mention only two). First, the student may pay attention to the 'facts' produced by the first speaker in one of the variety of ways suggested by existing courses. Secondly, the student may pay attention to the role of the second speaker – examine the second speaker's expressions of opinion and determine whether that second speaker is maintaining a consistent point of view or not. This, after all, is the sort of judgement native speakers make on each other when they say of someone, 'I can't pin him down', 'he's really slippery', etc.

One of the things that follows from deciding to use different sorts of texts for different purposes is that you no longer necessarily want texts which all take up the same amount of time. The teacher might use a few small snippets from conversations to illustrate some particular conversational gambit (cf. extracts (3.7)–(3.9)), then go on to play a more extended piece of interactional conversation to illustrate the use of this strategy, and then spend the last half of the lesson working with a fairly short transactional text where the students are required to complete a task. What seems to be required in course construction is a selection of strategies and tasks, exemplified in texts graded in the sort of way we have been describing, and a fairly fluid approach to the construction of a set of menus for each particular lesson, menus which may sometimes consist of a number of short extracts (particularly in the early stages) and may sometimes consist of a long blockbuster text whose content is made accessible to students by careful preparation and the judicious use of supports. In the next section we discuss and briefly exemplify the principles which underlie the notions 'careful preparation' and 'judicious support'.

3.7 Approaching a text

In this discussion of how one might use a chunk of taped conversational speech, we will suggest one way of using the material in such a way that the teacher can facilitate the student's interpretation of what he hears. The taped extract lasts about two minutes which is generally too long for a once-through listening exercise. The simple principle on which we've decided to divide up the extended chunk of speech is determined by the amount of *support* we think we can offer the student at the beginning of the listening exercise. Before the tape is played at all, the students should be provided with the map shown in figure 3.4. All the street and place names on this map are mentioned on the tape. Thus, a preliminary exercise involves familiarising the student with how these names are pronounced. If required, the conventions for reducing words like *road* (Rd), *terrace* (Terr.) can be illustrated, as indeed can the general conventions of map representation. As preparation for the type of information which will be heard on the tape, the teacher can ask the students how they would get from one location on the map to another. For example, 'describe how you would get from Lauder Road to Albert Terrace', or 'you live in Dick Place and go to school at George Watson's College, how would you walk to school in the morning?' If, in answering these questions, the students do not demonstrate a familiarity with expressions such as *go straight along, along, go over, get to, go up, walk along, down* (Lauder Road), then the teacher should take the opportunity to introduce these expressions and their typical uses. This should not, at this point, lead to a general lesson on these types of expressions. Rather, exemplification should be restricted to those expressions which will actually occur on the tape.

The amount of preliminary work required to provide support for the student will, of course, depend on the student's ability and previous experience of listening to spoken English. Having completed some preliminary work, the teacher can ask the students to listen to the tape and try to follow (or mark in pencil) the route which the speaker describes. It will help to tell them that the speaker will begin at the right-hand end of Grange Loan. The first brief piece of tape is transcribed here as extract (3.14). Only beginners should be provided with a transcript. For all other students, this has to be treated as a *listening*, and not a *reading* exercise.

(3.14) (6)   so the way I went was along Grange Lo- Gra- Grange Loan + em till it met + till you went over Whitehouse Loan + em + and then in fact straight along + Newbattle Terrace till you got to the Dominion + and then straight along Morningside whatever it is + to + the Tipperlinn gate of George Watson's College +

If the students had some difficulty with the speed of the description, then play the extract again. Emphasise, however, that they only have to be able to follow the route, not to hear and understand *every* word. If the students do have specific questions, arising from confusion over an expression such as *Morningside whatever it is*, the use of this vague form should be explained and its function in this context. This would be a good point to mention the alternative form *Blackford something or other* as fulfilling the same function. Try to

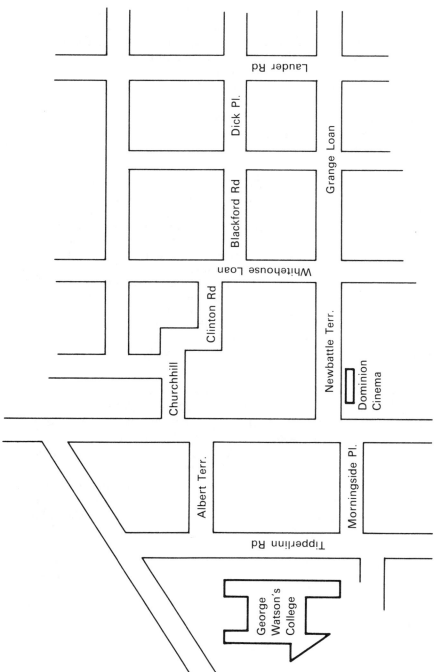

Figure 3.4

let what is explained, however, derive primarily from what the students feel they need to have explained, at this point.

In preparation for the next piece of tape to be listened to, the teacher should explain that the speaker is going on to describe the route he took back from George Watson's College. The speaker will describe a different route, which they should try to follow or mark in pencil, and he will give a reason for taking that route. So, the students have to listen for two things: the route description and the reason for taking that route. The next extract should then be played (twice, if the students require it).

(3.15) (7)   em + on the way back I used to come out the Tipperlinn Gate of George Watson's College + ah this was why I did it + I used to go up Albert Terrace + halfway up Albert Terrace I used to light up a cigarette + you see because that was a very quiet way to go + now when I'd lit up my cigarette I used to find myself at Churchhill + and the quickest way to get back from Churchhill + was to walk along long down Clinton Road + along Blackford something or other it's actually an extension of Dick Place but it's called + Blackford something or other it shouldn't be I mean it's miles away from Blackford Hill + but it's called Blackford Road I think + em + and then along to Lauder Road and down Lauder Road + which used to allow for the consumption of two cigarettes on the way back + +

The obvious teacher-questions involve the route and the reason the students think the speaker took that route. Apart from these questions, the teacher should try to let the after-listening discussion be determined by questions which the students need answers to, following what they have heard. A possible source of confusion is the section *Blackford something or other . . . Blackford Hill . . . Blackford Road I think*. An explanation of what is probably happening here seems relatively straightforward. The use of the word *consumption* may also give rise to some questions, which should be answered without extended discussion, at this point.

In preparation for the next brief extract, the teacher can explain that the speaker has not yet given his reason for taking that route when he wanted to smoke some cigarettes. The students could be asked what reasons they think he might have had and then asked to listen to the next piece of tape to find out if they were correct (fostering the element of prediction in interpretation).

(3.16) (8)   and also it was a road which no masters took + so I wasn't liable to be pulled out the next day + smoking on the way home +

With this brief extract, it is extremely likely that no student can make out all the actual words used. (Some native speakers disagree strongly on how it should be transcribed.) Yet, the meaning of what the speaker is saying as his reason for his route is not hard to grasp, and students should have no real difficulty. If students cannot guess who the *masters* refers to, then the term should be explained, briefly. We might note that the interpretation of this brief chunk of speech depends very much on our being able to construct an interpretation on the basis of background knowledge (schools often punish their pupils if caught smoking) or inference (students from this speaker's school are not allowed to smoke).

Once this extract has been discussed, and the students indicate that they know the routes taken and the reason the speaker took the return route, the teacher may ask the students if they heard another voice on the tape and whether that other person was a man or a woman. Do the students think what they have heard so far was the whole conversation between the two people? Of course not. So, there must be something before the speaker describes his route. What do the students think was said beforehand, to give rise to this route description?

Through some strategy comparable to the above, the teacher may then prepare his students to listen to the interactional dialogue which precedes the route description. The students should, by this stage, be familiar with the man's voice and not have too much difficulty distinguishing between the male and female voices in conversation. The point of keeping the two-speaker extract until last is that, from the listening comprehension point of view, it is a much less definable exercise. The 'content' of interactive conversation is generally much less specific than the 'content' of the route-description-plus-reason chunks which have been presented already. Once again, the student should not try to hear every word, but should try to listen for what the woman wants to know and what the man's response is. The man also gives a reason for his answer and the students can be asked to listen for this reason. The next extract on tape is transcribed as (3.17).

(3.17) (9)   A: and where did you go to school?
                 B: George Watson's College
                 A: for primary and secondary?
                 B: for primary and secondary yeah
                 A: right + em could you describe how you got from your home to the school + if you remember?
                 B: the exact route?
                 A: if you remember it
                 B: good grief what a funny question + yeah + yes I can +

A: (laughter)

B: erm + perfectly I mean absolutely perfectly 'cause I used to do it every day twice +used to walk it + I used to walk along Grange Loan + up Lauder Road ++ no no I didn't use to go that way I used to walk + this is going to be a ramified question I'm afraid

A: (laughter)

B: because I used to walk a different way from I used to go I used to have this +

A: oh hmm

B: well it's perfectly it's perfectly possible that one way + can + exert less energy than another +

A: yes

B: in opposite directions because you know hills

A: yes

B: you choose not to go up hills +

Teacher-questions should be concerned with what the woman wants to know (which school, how long, and what route the man took to school) and what answer the man gives and his reason. Student-questions may centre on the meaning of some expressions such as *primary and secondary, a ramified question* and *exert less energy*. The really troublesome expression is *a ramified question*. It may be suggested that the speaker intends to say that his answer will not be a simple one, but in aiming for *answer*, he has actually said *question*. (The man also says that *one way can exert less energy* which we have to interpret as meaning 'by going one way you can exert less energy'.) Difficult though it may be for foreign students to accept, the fact remains that native speakers often make 'mistakes', slips-of-the-tongue, when using English. Native listeners correspondingly compensate for such slips in their interpretations, since they are concerned with what the speaker intends to convey and not only with what the words alone convey. We would not expect a teacher to spend his time explaining this aspect of spoken production, at this point. His explanation may simply involve giving the student a more easily understood expression such as 'a long, complicated answer to your question'. If the students behave as if they have followed what is going on in this extract, the teacher can prepare them to listen to the whole two-minute extract straight through.

In this extended listening exercise, it would help the student, we believe, if he had some other purpose to his listening. There is certainly some benefit to be gained from listening to the complete version just to let the students become familiar with how all the separate chunks, which we have presented out of sequence, actually fit together. Let the student also think about some general aspects of this interaction while he is listening to the whole two minutes. For

example, the student may be asked to listen for parts where he thinks
the man is not sure what he is going to say next, and hesitates or
repeats himself. Or he may be asked to listen for the contributions
the woman makes. After all, she is in the 'listener role' for most of
this extract, but does she remain totally silent? Or if the teacher
wishes to present some comprehension questions of the traditional
type, we suggest that he put those on the blackboard *before* the
student listens to the full conversation again. If the teacher is
primarily interested in training his students to listen more effectively
to spoken English (and not testing them), it makes sense that he
should use his comprehension-style questions to direct the students'
attention while they are listening. In general, we would like to
suggest that a listening exercise should not simply be a passive
experience for a student (e.g. listening just to get used to hearing
English noises from native speakers). It should have a purpose. With
non-advanced students, we suggest that the structuring of the taped
data and the use of 'support' material, as we have exemplified briefly
here, may put the teacher in more of a training and facilitating role
than the more frequent 'testing' role he is required to assume in many
listening comprehension courses. So, armed with some purpose to his
having to listen to this whole piece of conversation, the student will
hear extract (3.18).

(3.18) (*10*)   A: and where did you go to school?
                B: George Watson's College
                A: for primary and secondary?
                B: for primary and secondary yeah
                A: right + em could you describe how you got from your
                      home to the school + if you remember?
                B: the exact route?
                A: if you remember it
                B: good grief what a funny question + yeah + yes I can +
                A: (laughter)
                B: erm + perfectly I mean absolutely perfectly 'cause I
                      used to do it every day twice + used to walk it + I used
                      to walk along Grange Loan + up Lauder Road + + no
                      no I didn't use to go that way I used to walk + this is
                      going to be a ramified question I'm afraid
                A: (laughter)
                B: because I used to walk a different way from I used to go
                      I used to have this + +
                A: oh hmm
                B: well its perfectly it's perfectly possible that one way +
                      can +exert less energy than another +
                A: yes
                B: in opposite directions because you know hills

A: yes
B: you choose not to go up hills + so the way I went was along Grange Lo- Gra- Grange Loan + em till it met + till you went over Whitehouse Loan + em + and then in fact straight along + Newbattle Terrace till you got to the Dominion + and then straight along Morningside whatever it is + to + the Tipperlinn Gate of George Watson's College + em + on the way back I used to come out the Tipperlinn Gate of George Watson's College + ah this was why I did it + I used to go up Albert Terrace + half way up Albert Terrace I used to light up a cigarette +
A: aha
B: you see because that was a very quiet way to go +
A: (laughter)
B: now when I'd lit up my cigarette I used to find myself at Churchhill – and the quickest way to get back from Churchhill – was to walk along long down Clinton Road + along + Blackford something or other it's actually an extension of Dick Place but it's called + Blackford something or other it shouldn't be I mean it's miles away from Blackford Hill +
A: (. . . . .)
B: but it's called Blackford Road I think + em + and then along to Lauder Road and down Lauder Road + which used to allow for the consumption of two cigarettes on the way back
A: aha
B: and also it was a road which no masters took +
A: ah
B: so I wasn't liable to be pulled out the next day +
A: (laughter)
B: smoking on the way home +
A: aha + so it was very well planned
B: it was it was it had to be
A: good

At this point, the teacher can ask for answers to the questions he put on the blackboard, or ask for opinions on the man's hesitations and repetitions, or about the woman's contributions to the conversation. It is up to the teacher how general he makes this final discussion and up to the students how much longer they're willing to show interest in this well-worked piece of conversational data.

For most students, the exercise format we have presented will be quite enough on the one piece of data. It will be time to listen to something else, something completely different. This does not mean that the teacher need abandon this piece of conversational data. He can return to it with the same student group, after a month or two, and use it to exemplify a number of features of spoken English which were ignored when the material was only used for a non-analytic listening comprehension purpose. There are several features of spoken English which we shall outline here and which the teacher can draw his students' attention to, in a more analytic approach to understanding what it is we are hearing when we listen to naturally occurring spoken English. We should emphasise again that we are using this one piece of data as a representative sample of spoken English production and that the specific examples we note here are to be treated as tokens of types of features which can be found, to a greater or lesser extent, in any spontaneous English speech. The teacher should be able to recognise other tokens in almost any conversational speech he has on tape.

1   Note the use of reduced forms of words which are normally found in the full form in written English – *'cause* (because) and *till* (until). Note also the frequency of the reduced forms – *it's, I'd, didn't, shouldn't, wasn't*. Such forms are often so reduced in the stream of speech that non-native listeners do not even hear them. They should be pointed out so that the student gets some practice at recognising them in their reduced forms.

2   Note that while *I* and *you* are used for the speaker and the listener respectively, there is also the occurrence of the very common generic use of *you* which is usually taken to mean 'people in general' and is believed to be equivalent to the more formal 'one'. In this case (as in many similar occurrences we have noted), the use of *you* actually has to be interpreted by the listener as referring to the speaker. It is being used in place of *I*.

3   Note the use of the 'fillers' – *I mean* (twice), *you know*. These expressions cannot just be thrown in anywhere in the stream of speech and frequently they are not interchangeable. On the two occasions this speaker uses *I mean*, he is about to give a reason for what he has just previously asserted. When he uses *you know*, he has already started to give his reason, using *because*, and the use of *you know* seems to be his indication that he expects the listener understands what he is about to say. For this speaker, in this extract, these two 'fillers' are used with meanings quite close to their literal meanings. When he talks about something for which he is the source of verification, he uses *I mean*. When he talks about something everyone (including the listener) will know about, he uses *you know*. Many speakers do not use these 'fillers' so consistently. Students should not be encouraged to use them a lot. It is much less distracting to hear a lot of the *em, erm,* and *mm*

type of filler than a lot of *you know* and *I mean* forms used inappropriately.

4 Note the occurrence of the *em, erm* type of filler. They are not frequent in this conversation, possibly because the speakers know that they can actually pause (as the man does quite often) without the other speaker jumping in and starting to speak. These forms are used by the man at points where he is taking time to plan what he will say next, especially when he is trying to remember the details of his route. Note that they occur within what would be fairly long pauses on four occasions (+ *em* +). In this type of speech situation, where their 'turn-holding' function is not really justified, they are possibly being used to avoid long silences. For most speakers of English, under normal circumstances, there appears to be a conventional avoidance of silence during conversations. For some non-native speakers from other cultures, this aspect of English speech takes a long time to get used to.

5 Note the use of pauses (marked by +). In the speech of the man, they often occur at syntactic boundaries, marking off phrases or sentence-like chunks. Occasionally they do not. When he is trying to remember his route, while continuing to speak, he produces chunks like + *can* +, + *to* +, and + *along* +. However, if one were to give students a means of identifying small chunks to listen to, in speech of this type, a useful, regularly small, chunk to pay attention to is the pause-bounded unit. Notice how often a small phrase is marked off by pauses: + *used to walk it* +, + *up Lauder Road* + + *the Tipperlinn Gate of George Watson's College* +; also, how often a very short sentence, with one piece of 'new' information, is marked off with pauses: + *I used to walk along Grange Loan* + + *till you went over Whitehouse Loan* +, + *ah this was why I did it* +, + *I used to go up Albert Terrace* +, and so on. Providing such a strategy for listening to speech seems much more appropriate than expecting students to listen for the type of sentence structures which are found in written language.

6 Note the uses of repetition: the use of repetition of part of a question as a means of answering the question (*for primary and secondary yeah*); the use of repetition to create planning time at the beginning of one's turn to speak (*well it's perfectly it's perfectly possible*); the use of repetition to make sure the listener is following the sequence of actions exactly (*now when I'd lit up my cigarette*); and the use of repetition for agreement with the previous speaker's statement (*it was it was*). This frequency of repetition is not at all a common feature in written language. Nor is the frequency of repetition of a particular structure, often with

the same verb – notice the number of times the man begins to describe something with *I used to . . . .*

7 Note the general use of 'paralinguistic' features, as described earlier on p. 61, which could lead to an extended discussion of what type of person the male speaker is, the relationship between the two speakers, and other non-verbal information to be gleaned from listening to a person speaking.

8 Notice that the speaker does not spell out everything he does, for example, in getting to school. He does not provide excessive detail such as 'I come out of my front door, walk down the path, open the gate, go out, close the gate.' Nor does he say that he turns right into Clinton Road, or that he crosses another road between Albert Terrace and Churchhill. Nor does he explain where *the Tipperlinn Gate* is – we can infer that this gate with such a name will be on Tipperlinn Road. Comprehension, then, requires some inferences. The range and number of inferences we are required to make, as listeners, depends to a large extent on how detailed we make our 'mental model' of the situation we hear described. For example, we can have a picture of the speaker, as a school student, appropriately dressed, walking along a sunny suburban street, with bushes, trees, other pedestrians, some traffic, and so on. This type of picture requires a 'depth of processing' of what we hear which is not a normal requirement of our everyday listening capacities. To carry out our listening comprehension via such elaborate models would probably make us very poor listeners, because we would become fixated with the suburban street scene and lose track of what the speaker has gone on to say next. Thus, we suggest that, if the notion of inference is brought into the discussion of understanding what one hears, it should be restricted, at first, to those 'necessary' inferences of a very simple type (such as *the Tipperlinn Gate* example). Consequently, when the lesson is primarily concerned with listening comprehension, it is best to avoid the type of so-called 'comprehension' question which takes the following form: 'The speaker says he passed the Dominion Cinema. Do you think the Cinema was open? Why?' This type of question may lead the students to think further about what they've been listening to, but it would be a mistake to think that it is a *listening* comprehension question.

3.8 Assessing listening comprehension

In the last section we outlined a method of approach to training in listening comprehension in the foreign language. In this approach the student is gradually prepared to encounter a spoken text, provided with all possible supports, and gradually exposed to crucial structured chunks. The *intention of the speaker in speaking* is constantly appealed to. Other, more analytic approaches, suitable for more advanced students to 'sensitise' them to typical details of spoken English were also illustrated.

It seems appropriate at this point to reiterate a conviction that we have expressed already several times earlier in the book. This is that it is hard to conceive what is meant by 'correct interpretation' of a spoken text. We have insisted that what is necessary is that each listener should construct a reasonable, hence coherent, interpretation of what is said. It must be obvious from the discussion in section 3.7 that, whereas we must assume that competent listeners will share some common 'gist' after listening to a chunk of spoken language, we should also expect that different listeners will reasonably extract different parts of the text as more 'salient' to them (perhaps because some particular piece of what is said appeals more vividly to their own experience), and so build their mental representations of 'what the text was about' around rather different structures. So one listener may build around a structure like 'my route to school', and another around a structure like 'smoking on the way home'. Choosing one rather than another will lead the listener to pay more attention to those features which are relevant to his view of what is going on, and less attention, *or none at all*, to features which do not relate to what he is interested in. Our real-life experience of chatting to friends, after listening to a lecture or watching a film, must be that people remember very different things as the details which are salient to them. If this is the normal process of interpretation, presumably it is that normal process which we wish foreign learners to acquire in listening to the target language.

It must be obvious that as soon as a 'testing' approach is introduced, the normal process flies out of the window. It is replaced by a demand that the student should learn to listen to those features which the tester has constructed his personal representation around. We shall return in chapter 4 to some consideration of assessing competence in listening comprehension. We make it clear now that we find existing approaches to the assessment of listening comprehension based on a very insecure theoretical notion of what 'comprehension' means. It is by no means clear that a great deal of what is currently tested in listening comprehension tests is necessary, or relevant, to the process of understanding the communicative event which the student has listened to. Whereas in assessing the comprehension of written language it might be argued that the *text* is available for checking against, so that questions on 'the text' are appropriate, it must be obvious that in assessing listening comprehension the *text* is not available to the student. What is available to him is his own personal representation of the *content* of the text, which is a very different matter. This representation is inside the student's head and is not directly available for extraction and objective examination. Any question or task required of the student requires first to be interpreted in its own right, and then matched up with the student's representation of the content of the text. This process must be extremely complex and we have, at present, no idea how to characterise it. Basic research on listening comprehension in extended texts is urgently required before any current methods of assessment can be regarded as appropriate diagnostic instruments and, in particular, before any current testing methodology can be regarded as providing a satisfactory motivation for constructing courses to teach listening comprehension in one way rather than another. Meanwhile, teachers should be very wary of general claims made about text comprehension which are based solely on results derived from experiments in which laboratory subjects listen to written sentences carefully read aloud. Such 'comprehension' reflects neither the type of material, nor the type of situation, which is involved in our normal listening. It may be disturbing, but it is nevertheless true, that we are still largely ignorant of what is involved in the process of interpreting language through 'normal listening'.

4 Assessing spoken language

4.0 Introduction

The assessment of the spoken language has traditionally been a headache for the English teacher. Many well-established tests do not even have an oral component, since grammatical accuracy and vocabulary can be assessed quite adequately, it seems, in the written mode. When an oral component is found in proficiency tests, it is often based on a discrimination between words which have very similar pronunciations. For example, the student hears a word spoken and has to decide whether the word he heard was *fairy*, *ferry* or *furry*. This type of sound recognition test may be useful in some situations, but it does seem to be a rather artificial activity. After all the student is unlikely to encounter many situations in which single words, totally without context, have to be understood. (One situation in which we all have difficulty in this regard is hearing someone's name for the first time, particularly if it is an unfamiliar surname. We inevitably need to hear it again.) The sound recognition test is an example of a form of assessment in which discrete elements in the language are tested one at a time, and the composite score of the student on these discrete items is taken as a measure of the student's general ability in coping with the sounds of English. Many more examples of this type of assessment methodology can be found in, for example, Robert Lado's book *Language Testing* (1961).

At quite the opposite extreme, the oral component of English language assessment may be based on a very general impression of how well the student speaks. This normally takes the form of an oral interview in which the examiner asks the student questions, or prompts the student to talk on certain, sometimes pre-arranged, topics. While the examiner also pays attention to aspects such as accent, grammar, vocabulary, and fluency in the student's speech, the overall score is often expressed as a point on a scale which has a definition such as 'able to satisfy routine social demands and limited work requirements'. This particular definition can be found as one rating used in *The Foreign Service Institute Oral Interview* which is discussed, along with other comparable oral test formats, in John Oller's book *Language Tests at School* (1979). The most general feature of this type of assessment is that it is carried out *as the student speaks* and is dependent on the examiner's maintaining a constant set of assessment criteria from the first student interviewed through to the fifty-first, and beyond. Since the oral interview is the most widely used form of assessment of spoken language abilities at the present time, it clearly has proved to be a useful tool in what is still generally considered a problem area of assessment.

Rather than present a survey of types of tests and their problems (the reader may consult Oller 1979 or J. B. Heaton's *Writing English Language Tests*, 1976), we prefer to present some basic principles and some practical examples which the classroom teacher may find more useful than a general test format when he wishes to assess the spoken language abilities of his students. As we have emphasised elsewhere in this book, our suggestions are not intended as an alternative to a teacher's current practice, but are presented as supplementary. They are designed to give the teacher more options, both in how he teaches and in how he assesses the spoken language.

4.1 Assessing spoken English production

Naturally, there will continue to be a requirement that students be assessed on their command of the grammar and vocabulary which they have been taught. Teachers may also wish to make informed judgments on the pronunciation and fluency of their students' speech. We suggest that the teacher should continue to assess these features, not in isolation, but as part of his assessment of the student's ability to communicate effectively in the spoken mode. Communicating effectively is clearly a feature of primarily transactional rather than primarily interactional speech, as we defined these terms earlier. We have suggested that one of the main aims of most English teachers is to make their students able to communicate information effectively in spoken English. In pursuing this aim, the teacher may wish to be able to assess, at regular intervals, how his students are progressing and also to find out if there are areas of performance which are consistently weak and require additional attention. What kind of methodology would be appropriate to this type of assessment?

We shall suggest first a number of practical requirements, and then set out some guiding principles which underlie a methodology for the assessment of spoken English production.

4.2 Practical requirements

An assessment profile

There is a tendency to treat assessment as a once-a-term or once-a-year activity. The student takes *the* test, such as an 'O' level examination or Cambridge Proficiency on a particular day, and his performance in that test, on that day, is taken to be a standard measure of the student's ability. This seems a particularly inappropriate method of assessing a student's spoken language skills. It would be both more informative for the teacher and fairer to the student to have some continuous record of the student's spoken performance on different occasions and for different purposes. This approach is sometimes described as 'formative' assessment and is distinguished from the 'summative' assessment undertaken in the once-a-year exam. In order to maintain an assessment record of a student's spoken performance, the teacher need only use an informal chart with headings reflecting those aspects of the student's speech which the teacher feels confident of measuring. The chart may take the form presented in figure 4.1.

Date	Type of speech required	Grammatical correctness	Appropriate vocabulary	Fluency/ pronunciation	Information transfer score	Others

Figure 4.1

Some of the categories shown in figure 4.1 ('fluency' for example) will have to be assessed through subjective judgments by the teacher. It is usually thought that subjective judgments are unreliable and liable to substantial variation. However, such judgments, made by a competent teacher who is, after all, the best-informed judge of what his own students have been taught (and should know), can provide a valid basis for informal assessment. We will concentrate, in the discussion which follows, on providing a basis for a more objective means of assessment. We must emphasise, however, that we do not suggest that the objective approach should override the teacher's subjective assessment. The two types of assessment should be used to arrive at a fuller characterisation of the student's performance. Given this basic chart for recording comments or scores on a student's performance, what else should be included in the student's assessment profile? In addition to a record of assessment, it would make sense to retain some record of what that assessment is based on – that is, the student's spoken performance.

The student's tape

Most assessment of spoken English is undertaken as the student speaks. We must assume that this is an administrative rather than a pedagogical convenience. It seems a monumental task to pay attention simultaneously to all the features listed as headings in figure 4.1.

It makes a lot more sense to tape-record the student as he speaks, if only as a means of checking, at a later stage, whether the initial impressions were correct. Moreover, the provision of a tape for each student can provide several other benefits. From an assessment point of view, the taped performance of a student can be kept as evidence to support the teacher's judgments. It is available for checking by others if the teacher is unsure about assigning a score or grade to a particular student. If the student records a number of performances on the same tape over a period of weeks or months, the teacher can check over those performances and gain an impression of whether the student has improved or not. He can, moreover, illustrate any improvement both to outside observers and, perhaps more importantly, to the student himself.

This last point may be seen as one of the pedagogical advantages to be derived from maintaining a taped record of a student's spoken performance. Many students forget how they performed, say, a month or two earlier, and often feel that they are not making any advances in their use of English. If an earlier (hesitant, ungrammatical or confused) version of a story-telling can be played back and compared with a more recent (more competent) version, then the student may gain some confidence that the work and exercises of the classroom are beneficial and worthwhile.

The taped record may also be used more immediately for diagnostic purposes. If the teacher forms the impression that a particular student seems to be making a consistent error of some sort, then he can listen to the tape for specific examples. Having identified some examples, he can illustrate the problem to the particular student and suggest ways in which the student may overcome the identified difficulty. Alternatively, if the teacher finds a general type of error is occurring among the performances of his student group, he can use his taped examples as an introductory 'how not to' part of a lesson which goes on to suggest ways of 'how to' express some particular aspect of the English language. Such a pedagogical strategy has much to recommend it. Students, like most other people, tend to be much more interested in what *they* say, rather than what some character in a course-provided tape says. This principle, of encouraging the student to pay attention to his own performance, has become more widely used in teaching written production, even for native speakers of English. It can only be implemented for spoken production, if a taped record of (at least some of) the student's talk is maintained.

Finally, if a consistent record of a student's spoken performance is maintained, the idea of the once-a-year test may become obsolete. If some external examiner wishes to assess the student's spoken language skills, either for the purposes of external certification or as an inspection of the institution's standards, he has available a record of every student's performance. He can check for progress, or for performance in a specific type of speech activity (story-telling, for example), as well as listening to the most recent performance for all the traditional features such as grammatical accuracy and use of vocabulary.

We suggest that the maintenance of a taped record of samples of a student's spoken English production is crucial in any serious approach to the assessment of spoken English. We are aware that maintaining a taped record and doing some assessment on the basis of this taped record will require more of the teacher's time than has been typically devoted to spoken English assessment in the past. Yet the time involved need not be any more than is normally devoted to checking samples of students' written work, such as essays. It is a question of how seriously the production of spoken English is treated within a syllabus which also incorporates the production of written English. For different student groups, the balance between spoken and written work will vary. However, we stress the point that if spoken language production is considered a necessary part of the teaching syllabus, then its assessment should be taken seriously. In order to carry out effective assessment, a student profile containing a student's tape is a basic practical requirement.

Given that each student is to produce a tape, what type of material should be recorded? Clearly it would be a waste of resources to record every English-like noise which emanates from the student. Rather, the student should be prepared to talk, and be recorded, on a limited number of occasions during a session. He should also be required to produce talk in different modes and not be allowed to produce a story, for example, on every occasion. In the next two sections, we shall suggest general categories of types of speech and ways of eliciting speech in different modes.

Speech in different modes

We have already proposed, in chapter 2, that there are variable degrees of difficulty inherently present in different types of speaking. Taking short turns is generally easier than long turns. Talking to a familiar, sympathetic, individual is less demanding than talking to an unfamiliar, uninvolved individual or group. Something one knows about and has well-organised in memory is naturally easier to talk about than a new topic or an experience which has little internal organisation in itself. Bearing these distinctions in mind, the teacher should be able to judge what type of speaking activity the student would find reasonably 'unstressful' at a particular point in his course. Deciding what speech activity the student will record has to be determined in terms of the level of communicative stress which the teacher believes the student can cope with, at a particular point.

Perhaps it should also be borne in mind that even native speakers of English find that a straight description is easier, in some sense, than telling a story and, in turn, that telling a story is easier than a justification of an opinion. This is a rather general guide to level of difficulty. Naturally, a short narrative involving a single character and only two or three events may be easier than a lengthy description covering many details and relationships. Let us try to capture this general differentiation between modes of speech in a fairly informal grid, as shown in figure 4.2.

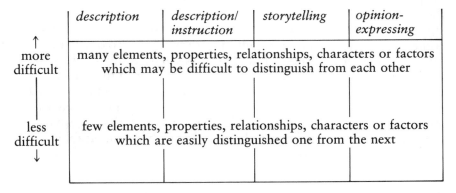

	description	description/ instruction	storytelling	opinion- expressing
↑ more difficult	many elements, properties, relationships, characters or factors which may be difficult to distinguish from each other			
less difficult ↓	few elements, properties, relationships, characters or factors which are easily distinguished one from the next			

Figure 4.2

The grid in figure 4.2 is organised around the speech modes rather than the written modes. It is presented in this way in order to show that if the teacher can control some of the interactive parameters mentioned earlier, then he can also use the grid to control, to some extent, the level of difficulty of the *content* of the speech activity. In a school or college, controlling the interactive parameters should be relatively easy. The teacher can make sure that each student has a comparable listener. (We shall have more to say on the status of the listener below, pp. 111–12.) The length of turn required can be set as brief or extended, according to the type of speech activity selected from the grid in figure 4.2.

What we hope the grid in figure 4.2 will ensure is that the student is given the opportunity to produce different types of speech and is not always recorded performing in a single mode. Giving instructions on how to do something requires different structures and often quite different vocabulary from relating a sequence of events involving two or three characters. It is quite possible that a student who can cope easily, for a variety of background reasons, with relating a complex sequence of events, has great difficulty producing even a brief set of instructions on how to do something. If the teacher can use this assessment methodology to discover such gaps in his students' spoken English abilities, then it clearly has a valuable function in assisting the teacher to decide what to emphasise in his teaching.

The practical requirement we have emphasised here is the assessment of the student's ability to perform in a variety of speech modes. What we have not determined is how the teacher can ensure that the student does produce speech of the required type. Nor have we provided any means by which the teacher can make the student talk about what the teacher wants him to talk about, for assessment purposes. One of the key problems in assessing spoken production is the difficulty in assessing, with some constancy of criteria, one student describing a painting, another student describing the town he comes from, another describing his motorcycle, and so on. They are all producing 'descriptions', but the criteria of assessment which are applied may differ according to the subject-matter. If the teacher wishes to ensure that he can be consistent in the criteria he applies, it helps enormously if he can pre-determine the speech task for all the students in a group. If the teacher has a set of task types, he can elicit the required type of speech and be sure that he has comparable speech from all his students.

Task types

The practical requirement which is met by a task-based approach to the assessment of spoken production is that there should be some *constancy of elicitation input*. That is, every student is asked to do the same thing. This is, after all, the norm in most other test formats. One does not normally ask students to indicate which grammatical structures and vocabulary items they would choose to have examined in a test. The examiner decides on a set of questions and asks every student to provide answers to this set. The task-based approach, however, is not as strict on detail as the traditional test of grammar and vocabulary. Rather, it provides, in the form of a specific task, a general requirement that the speaker perform the task, using spoken English, but does not demand that he use any specific grammatical structures or any specific vocabulary items in his performance. Those structures and words he does choose to use, however, must be adequate for the performance of the task.

We have already listed some speech modes such as description and story-telling, in the informal grid in figure 4.2. We can now incorporate these speech modes within a taxonomy of task types and suggest some practical elicitation materials to be used in the tasks.

The type of speech required in producing a description or a set of instructions is essentially an account of fixed or static relationships. The properties of an object or the relationship of one object to another tend to be stable. In a story-telling task, however, the relationships tend to be dynamic. That is, there are changes of character, location and time involved, and the activities of the characters will typically differ as the story progresses. In expressing an opinion, there tends to be quite a different set of relationships, mainly abstract, between one part of what is being talked about and the next. These aspects of task types are summarised below. We can say that tasks are used to elicit spoken accounts of:

1 *Static relationships*
   (i)   Describing an object or photograph
   (ii) Instructing someone to draw a diagram
   (iii) Instructing someone how to assemble a piece of equipment
   (iv) Describing/instructing how a number of objects are to be arranged
   (v)   Giving route directions
2 *Dynamic relationships*
   (i)   Story-telling
   (ii) Giving an eye-witness account
3 *Abstract relationships*
   (i)   Opinion-expressing
   (ii) Justifying a course of action

Some of the materials which can be used in these task types are not difficult to prepare. Objects to be described can range from the everyday objects in the classroom to quite unfamiliar objects (e.g. the jointed metal links used to connect scaffolding pipes together). Diagrams with lines, circles, squares and triangles in some arrangement are easily drawn and can be presented in endless variations. Pieces of equipment may be more difficult to procure, but describing the assembly and use of even quite simple pieces of equipment can present unexpected difficulties for speakers. Think of how you would go about instructing someone, using only the spoken language, how to wire an electric plug, use a tin opener, put staples into a stapler, plait someone's hair, etc. The description of how a number of objects is arranged is actually a familiar activity, and can work with made-up arrangements of pencils, rubbers and books, or with culturally-fixed arrangements such as place-settings at a dinner table (e.g. in a photograph). The giving of route directions is also a familiar activity and can be done with simplified maps, actual street maps or even with plans of the London Underground system.

Story-telling can be prompted with cartoon-strips, sequences of photographs or, if facilities are available, with short pieces of film or video. Similar material input, such as a piece of film showing a crime being committed or a traffic accident, can be used to elicit eye-witness accounts. Prompts for eliciting opinions may range from a set of pictures of different houses, differently furnished rooms, different cars, holiday locations, etc., accompanied by the questions, 'Which do you prefer? and why?'. Alternatively, posters or advertisements may be presented for the student's opinion. Another method, which is rather more difficult to prepare, involves finding a piece of video or film in which someone expresses a strong opinion on an issue and showing it to the student, followed by a 'what do you think about that?' question. Justifying a course of action can be elicited by pictures, or a short piece of film, of an individual in some situational dilemma which does not show a solution and having the student provide and justify his solution.

This is a general list which is intended as an illustration of the types of materials which can be employed. The practising teacher will no doubt be able to add to the list examples of materials which, in his experience, have proved effective in eliciting talk from students. We shall present illustrative examples for each section of the taxonomy in section 4.4. So far we have described task types to elicit talk from the student, but we have not provided the student with a purpose for his talk. Certainly, these task types can be used as classroom exercises with no definable purpose other than the practice of 'speaking English' for its own sake. For assessment purposes, however, there is an often neglected practical requirement in eliciting spoken English production. The purpose of the elicited talk must be clear to the student. In order to have a purpose for speaking, the student must know who he is talking to and what his listener knows. If the listener knows the same as (or even more than) the speaker about an object, then what would be the point of the speaker's describing that object?

The information gap

If a teacher places an orange on a table in front of a foreign student and asks 'What is that?', he may be behaving in accordance with some established pedagogical methodology. If he did the same thing outside the classroom with another native speaker of English, he might be considered to be behaving in an odd manner. What is the difference between these two situations? We might say that the difference is to do with the conventions for asking questions. In normal life, we generally do not ask questions which have patently obvious answers. By the same token, we do not normally tell people what they quite obviously know already. We are usually motivated to tell people things we assume they do not know. It also helps, in normal behaviour, if the listener actually wants or needs to know what the speaker is communicating.

If we incorporate these normal behaviour principles into our assessment procedures, then we clearly do not want the student to be recorded talking (describing, instructing, story-telling, etc.) to his teacher. The established status of the teacher is that he knows more than the student about most things encountered in the learning situation. If the teacher gives the student an object to describe, then the student has to create, *for himself*, an artificial information gap between his knowledge and the teacher's. He has to behave as if the teacher doesn't know what the object looks like. Why should we require this additional, and highly artificial, dimension in the student's behaviour, when it is only his ability to use spoken English which we wish to assess?

In eliciting spoken production for assessment, we should make sure that the speaker can see a reasonable purpose for performing the task at hand. There should be a listener who does not have the information which the speaker has, and who needs that information. This can be simply achieved by having another student take the role of listener. In his role as listener, the second student also has some task to perform which depends upon his receiving information from the speaker. For example, the speaker is provided with a simple drawing of a line, a square and a triangle on a page. The listener cannot see the drawing, but is provided with a pen and a sheet of blank paper. A small, but identifiable, information gap has been created. The speaker's task is to instruct the listener to reproduce, as accurately as possible, the drawing which he can see, but the listener cannot. This technique can, of course, be used with one student speaking and the whole of the rest of the class as listeners.

The tasks we have described for the speaker to perform also provide a variety of tasks for the listener. In a description task, the speaker may be provided with one photograph to describe and the listener with a set of four or five similar photographs, only one of which is exactly the same as the speaker's. On the basis of the speaker's description, the listener tries to choose the correct photograph. In a story-telling task, the listener may have a set of pictures showing ten characters or ten scenes. He has to identify those pictures which fit the story the speaker is telling. Alternatively, he may have a set of some pictures which, properly arranged, would fit the sequence of events in the story. Paying attention to the speaker's account of what happened, if it is effective, will enable the listener to complete his task.

The requirement that the speaker's account be 'effective' was mentioned in connection with the listener's performing his task. In a sense, the task-based approach is ideally designed to assess 'communicative effectiveness', for it provides a limited amount of information to be communicated, a listener who needs to have that information communicated to him, and a taped record which the teacher can use when he comes to assign a grade to the student's performance. This leads us to the final practical requirement in the assessment of spoken language production – a set of scoring procedures for the tasks.

Scoring procedures

It might seem, at first glance, to be obvious how we could assess 'communicative effectiveness' in the performance of these tasks. We only have to check if the listener was able to perform his task correctly. There is, however, an obvious danger in using this criterion. The listener may, by chance or intelligence, arrive at a correct solution to his task, quite independently of what the speaker says. Alternatively, the listener may, from poor understanding, poor hearing or poor intelligence, arrive at a wrong solution to his task, again regardless of how the speaker has performed. The listener may even get something small wrong early in the task and then interpret everything which follows in the light of this initial mistake. As assessors, how would we know if this was, in fact, the case? Even if we could depend on the listener to perform his task competently, we could only say that, on the basis of the listener's performance, this speaker did, or did not, produce an effective piece of spoken English communication. We could not grade the performance as a 'four out of ten' or an 'eight out of ten' for example. We could only say it was 'ten', or 'zero', out of ten. Perhaps, more importantly, we would not be able to make diagnostic judgments about the speaker's performance. We could not say this speaker lost points in this version of the task because he failed to mention certain details, such as the location of the square, or that the man in the story went out to a disco. Since it would be an advantage to be able to point to such specific aspects of spoken performance, it would prove extremely useful to have some more detailed scoring method than the 'yes/no' switch provided by what the listener does.

One scoring procedure which could obviously be used is one which teachers traditionally employ on students' written production. This is probably best characterised as an 'error-based' form of assessment. The teacher allocates ten points for performance on the task, and deducts one point each time an error of grammar, pronunciation or vocabulary is made. Thus, the following fragment from a version of a story, transcribed as it sounded, would probably lose three points, for having *went* instead of 'gone', *oot* instead of 'out' and *party* instead of 'disco': *The man's got ready and he's went oot to a party.*

Certainly, an advantage of having the taped record of the student's performance is that it allows the teacher to carry out this type of 'error-based' scoring in a consistent and thorough way for the whole student group. If a pattern of grammatical errors (wrong past participle forms) or misused vocabulary (using *party* too generally) is discerned, then the teacher can use his observations as a basis for some revision work on points which his students have forgotten.

However, the teacher may not actually have assessed any aspect of how 'communicatively effective' the performance was. Although the example quoted already has three 'errors', it may have been an adequate piece of communication on that particular occasion. So, we might make a distinction between 'error-based' scoring for measuring success in using the formally correct aspects of the language, and 'required-information-based' scoring for measuring success in using the language to communicate effectively. Since the identification of grammatical error is a relatively easy and familiar activity for the English language teacher, we shall devote our attention to the less familiar business of scoring for 'required information'.

The fact that a 'required information' scoring technique has not been adequately formulated in the past is due largely to the rather haphazard selection of materials used in eliciting spoken production for assessment. If the student is asked to talk for one (or two or five) minutes on a topic, then it is hard to decide what the student is *required* to communicate to his listener. In such an exercise, the student may communicate a lot of information, but he may miss out some information which his listener needs. The teacher, however, has no consistent basis for judging what is necessary and what is unnecessary information. Similarly, if a strip-cartoon story is placed between the examiner and the student for the student to produce 'a story', the examiner does not have a reliable basis for saying the student produced an account in which all the required information was communicated. In this quite common assessment scenario, there is, in effect, no 'required information' to be communicated, since the listener (the examiner) already has access to all the information he requires in order to understand the story.

We have suggested two basic practical requirements in the assessment of spoken production. There should be a set of task types and there should be an information gap between what the speaker knows and what his listener knows. Given these two elements, the 'required information' scoring procedure is relatively straight-forward. The teacher checks the task material input and lists the elements which the listener needs to know. As an example of how this is done, consider what the listener needs to know in a diagram-drawing task. The listener has a blank sheet of paper, a red pen and a black pen. What the speaker has to communicate is the information necessary for the listener to reproduce, as accurately as possible, the diagram which the speaker (alone) can see. The list of required details for one such task is presented in figure 4.3.

The 'required information' in such a task is not, it should be emphasised, the same thing as the 'required vocabulary'. If the speaker says *box* instead of *square*, or *one inch* instead of *two centimeters*, *underneath* or *below* or *down from* instead of *under*, then he is performing perfectly adequately. Nor should strict mathematical accuracy be required (unless that is an additional purpose of the assessment) since saying *a little bit down from the square* will be just as effective in these circumstances as *one centimeter under the square*. The aim in a task of this sort is to define the 'required information' and to allow the student to use *what language he has* to communicate that 'required information'. This latter point can perhaps be better illustrated with some extracts from a task which involves assembling a piece of (to most people) unfamiliar equipment.

The speaker was shown (by gesture and deictic expressions) how to assemble a part of a mincer. He was given a photograph with the mincer disassembled and a number beside each component part to remind him of the sequence in which the parts were to be put together to reassemble the mincer. See illustration 5 (p. 154 below).

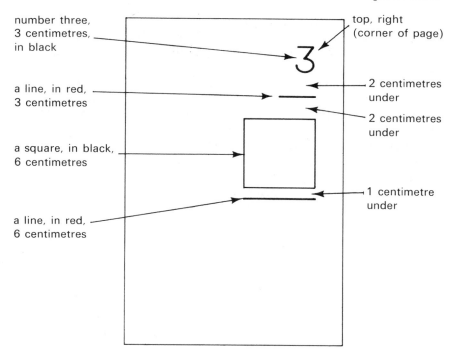

Figure 4.3

The listener had the various pieces of the mincer in front of him and was required to assemble it, following carefully the speaker's instructions. The speaker could not see what the listener was doing.

This task requires the speaker to present information in an instructional (+ descriptive) mode, and is similar to the diagram-drawing task. The difference between the two tasks is that the mincer task is less 'abstract' than the diagram-drawing task and may be closer to a 'real-world' situation in which information about putting something together must be conveyed through speaking. It also seems to be more fun for students.

The 'required information' is, once again, the identification of the separate components and the relationships between those components (how they fit together). The vocabulary used can be whatever expressions adequately serve to identify the components involved. Thus, the first part has been described as: *the biggest part, the bit that looks like a gun, the big L-shape piece, the piece – like a hairdryer.* The second part is effectively identified by the following range of expressions used by students: *the spiral, the long curly thing, the drill part, the sort of corkscrew piece.* The point we would like to emphasise is that most native speakers of English would not have the technically correct vocabulary for describing these components. They would have to use appropriate descriptive phrases. The requirement of the non-native speaker performing this task should accordingly be that he produces any description which identifies the object he is referring to. This fits in with a point we made earlier, in chapter 2, that students should be encouraged to work with whatever language they have, to manipulate it, to meet their communicative purposes. Like native speakers, they cannot be expected to have exactly the right vocabulary item in every situation.

To illustrate how the mincer task can be scored for 'required information', we shall present three transcribed extracts of speakers performing the beginning of the task and a set of scores in figure 4.4. The requirements here are that the first two components be adequately identified and the relationship between them be described. It must also be made clear which part of the second component is 'fitted into' which part of the first. Thus, there are five 'required information' points to be scored in these three versions.

(a) the part that looks like a gun that's the first one + then you've got the second part's a drill + and then you fit it in

(b) the big curly bit with the biggest bit going in first

(c) take your biggest part + and hold it with the biggest ring + the widest end facing upwards to the roof + and get your bit with the + like a screw + and + put it in with the square end at the bottom

Required information	Extracts		
	(a)	(b)	(c)
component (1)	√		√
component (2)	√	√	√
relationship (2 → 1)	√	√	√
connecting part of (1)			√
connecting part of (2)		√	√

Figure 4.4

The basic scoring procedure presented in figure 4.4 should give some indication of the way 'required information' can be scored. Notice that it allows the teacher to award a positive score for the amount of information effectively communicated. It also provides the teacher with an opportunity to show the speaker of (b) exactly how her performance has been inadequate in specific details. In fact, once a particular task has been used with a group of pupils and the teacher has identified specific failings in particular performances, he has available a useful resource for illustrating 'communicative ineffectiveness' to other students. If he plays a taped performance which does not make clear to the listener what he has to do, the listening student should be able to recognise, for himself, what problems are encountered with inexplicit communications. We believe that the basic scoring procedures which we suggest could, in fact, be carried out by some groups of advanced students themselves.

We should also point out that, by operating the task-based elicitation procedure, the teacher is not only eliciting spoken performances in English which can be scored for 'required information'. He is providing himself with a set of taped performances elicited under conditions which he is thoroughly familiar with and which are constant for his whole student group. He has an excellent set of data for also considering his students' use of specific grammatical structures and specific vocabulary. He knows, unlike his colleagues who simply listen to their students talking about 'my hobby' or 'my weekend', what it is the students are *trying* to say. He can also study his taped data-base for pronunciation or fluency or whatever other aspects of language use he feels are relevant.

In this section we have presented an introduction to the scoring of spoken English production on two tasks. Having described the practical requirements for assessment, we shall in section 4.3 explicitly set out the principles which underlie this methodology. We shall then, in section 4.4, present extended exemplification of how these scoring procedures can be applied, for various purposes, on all the task types we have discussed.

4.3 Principles underlying the methodology

Elicit speech which has a purpose

This principle is far too often ignored, not only in language assessment, but in classroom exercises too. For some reason, the use of drills, so popular in 'direct method' approaches, has remained the rather unimaginative solution to the problem of how to get students to speak. Yet a drill is the archetypal form of speech for no purpose and for no listener. We suggest that it must be better, and much more motivating, for the student to have a listener who needs to know something which the speaker knows. If the student has a purpose in speaking, he immediately finds himself in a situation in which what he says and how he says it have significance. In such a situation, it *counts* whether he uses the language effectively and accurately, or not. If he performs badly, someone will be unable to carry out a task and will, no doubt, complain. If he performs well, he has immediate feedback that something has been accomplished by him through the use of the language he has been learning.

Elicit extended chunks of speech

In beginners' courses we have suggested that the interactive short turn is a useful thing to learn. Yet, as the student progresses, it is noticeable that, while he is gradually being asked to produce more extended pieces of written work, the length of the spoken English turns he is required to produce is not extended in the same way. He is required only to answer questions or to provide complete sentences from various inputs. Many foreign language students who can produce lengthy written essays in examinations are never asked to produce more than a couple of sentences of speech. We suggest that, unless the student only really needs written English skills, he should be prepared to speak at length. The task-based approach creates situations in which the speaker has to produce extended chunks of speech. If used in teaching the intermediate and advanced student, it can give the student practice in putting together all that he has learned (in sentential terms) to produce discourse in the foreign language. If used in assessment, it provides the examiner with an opportunity to assess what the student can do when he 'has the floor' and is in charge of communication. All too often in the interview type test, the student is in the subordinate position, has only to provide answers to questions and is required to tell the examiner what the examiner clearly knows already. Requiring only short chunks of speech from a student is one effective means of preventing the student from becoming able to use the foreign language with any confidence in speaking outside the classroom. Requiring extended chunks of speech, with support from the inherent structure of a specific task, will give the student experience in being in charge in the speech situation and responsible for effective communication taking place. This seems a better preparation for talking with confidence in a foreign language than only practising what to say when asked a question or repeating a drill pattern of the structure of single sentences.

Elicit structured or organised speech

When we suggest that extended samples of speech should be elicited from the student, we do not intend that the teacher should be satisfied with *any* lengthy production of English speech by a student. After all, there are some students who do not need to be motivated to talk, they can produce an endless stream of talk quite readily. Such talk is often rambling, incoherent, and not particularly effective in communicative terms. Instead, we suggest that, as far as possible, the student should be encouraged to produce speech which is effectively organised so that the listener does not have to do a lot of 'work' trying to follow what is being said. Since organising what one wants to say is not always a simple procedure, even for native speakers of English, it is extremely helpful if there is some external structure in the information to be communicated which can be used as support in organising the spoken message.

In the tasks we have described, there is a variable amount of inherent structure or sequencing which can be used in the structure or sequencing of the descriptions, instructions, or narratives produced. In the mincer task, the student can see where to begin, what has to be described before what, and where to end. Of course, if the student becomes adept at this type of task, the teacher can gradually remove some of the external-structure prompts and check whether the student has actually developed the linguistic structuring required. That is, the component parts of a piece of equipment may be presented in a jumble, with no indication of the assembly sequence in the photographic prompt, or the photographic prompt itself can finally be removed, leaving the student to organise what he has to say from memory. What is being manipulated in these changes to the task input is the degree of 'communicative stress' which the student has to cope with. We suggest that the student should not be faced with any more 'communicative stress' than is appropriate to his stage of learning.

If the student needs external structure, such as is presented by the tasks we have described, in order to gain experience in structuring his message, then he should be provided with it. It must be a rare student who actually *wants* to produce rambling, unstructured bits and pieces of language in a response to a question such as 'What do you think about nuclear power?' This is not an easy question to answer, since there is little salient external structure on which to base the response. Perhaps the student would be better able to organise and present a coherent answer to this type of question after he had developed an ability to produce extended talk on a graded set of tasks which have variable amounts of externally structured support. We will illustrate some tasks within this graded set, ranging from the simple diagram-drawing task (a lot of external support) to the opinion-expressing task (much less external support). The purpose of these tasks is not, of course, to make students 'good' at describing diagrams, for example; it is to provide the student with something to say, and a basis for organising what he has to say.

Control the input

One of the possible disadvantages of the interview format as a means of assessing spoken language skills is that the examiner can rarely be sure that what the student produces as an answer is, in fact, an answer to the question at hand. The illusion that is maintained is that the student and the interviewer are having some form of spontaneous interaction, using the spoken language. This is a necessary illusion, since only by adhering to it can the examiner justifiably claim that his assessment represents an assessment of the student's ability to talk, in a one-to-one situation, in French or English or whatever language is being assessed. However, if the student predicts (or indeed is specifically informed) that he is likely to be asked some question on a recent holiday or a book he has read, he can 'prepare' his answer. Typically, he will write out a set of sentences, possibly with the help of his teacher, and 'learn' this set of written sentences as a prepared answer, should such a question arise in the interview. Given this scenario, the examiner has no way of knowing whether the student is an extremely able, spontaneous speaker of the language or simply has a good memory for limited chunks of prepared material. The problem is essentially that, in the typical interview situation, the examiner does not control the input (or the content) of what the speaker will say. He cannot even know if the holiday being so perfectly described was, in fact, taken by the student sitting across the table from him.

In the task-based approach, the examiner decides what the student has to talk about. The task(s) on which the student has to perform may be generally familiar in form to the student, but the student cannot 'prepare' a written version of what he will say. That is, although the student may anticipate that he will have to describe a diagram, he does not know beforehand whether there is a triangle, a square, or a circle, next to, under, down to the right of, a short red line, a black square of about five centimetres, and so on. The examiner determines what has to be described. The same principle applies in the other types of task. What the examiner (or the teacher taking the role of examiner) wants to know when testing a student is not whether the student has learned a routine for one particular diagram arrangement or one specific cartoon-strip, but whether the student has the general ability to produce an extended piece of spoken English appropriate to the communicative situation he encounters.

In a teaching exercise using a version of one of these tasks, the teacher can provide vocabulary, structures, suggest strategies for description or narration, and generally offer a lot of support. In a test, the student is required to demonstrate that he has learned to use, not to repeat, what he has been taught.

Quantify the notion of 'communicative effectiveness'

The widespread interest in teaching language, not simply as a set of correct forms, but as a means of communication, has put a premium on the notion of 'communicative effectiveness' in the student's use of the language. One of the serious problems which teachers using the communicative approach have encountered is the difficulty of assessing the abilities of students taught in this way. The task-based approach offers at least a partial solution to this problem. It cannot offer guidelines for deciding when a warning or a promise has been felicitously performed in English, but it can provide a basic scoring procedure for determining how much 'required information' was effectively communicated. The score achieved by the student on a particular task is expressed in terms of the positive number of points of required information which were expressed. The level of precision required by the teacher, or his institution, in the descriptions produced by the student can be set as a number of points to be gained. Such score levels can be established within an institution as the criteria on which decisions about subsequent training can be made.

There is also within the task-based approach a measure of grading on the basis of cognitive difficulty which can be used in addition to the quantification of performance on a particular task. Within each task type there can be 'easy' and 'more difficult' tasks. We have illustrated a relatively easy version of the diagram-drawing task in figure 4.3. It should be apparent that more complex arrangements with more elements and more complicated interrelationships would constitute a more difficult version of the same task type. Describing the wiring of a circuit board would generally be a more difficult task than the wiring of an ordinary domestic electric plug. Giving an eye-witness account of a traffic accident involving five cars would present greater difficulties than a two-car crash. The more complex the cognitive problem for the student, the greater the demand that he should exhibit conscious and specific control of the linguistic forms which he is using to communicate with. Thus, the tasks themselves can be organised into a graded series which provides a basis for assessment and consequently for decisions about abilities, progress and future training.

In the next section we will illustrate in detail how the scoring procedures operate on performances we have recorded. The general approach we have advocated in our discussion of assessing spoken production may best be summed up in the following quotation from John Oller: 'We seek testing procedures that provide the crucial props of something to say and someone to say it to, or at least that faithfully reflect situations in which such factors are present' (Oller, 1979: p. 305).

4.4 Task types and scoring procedures

In this section we shall present detailed examples of task types, data extracts and scoring procedures. We emphasise that these examples should be treated as suggested guidelines and should be considered critically. They are not presented as 'solutions' of any kind. If they present the teacher with a basis for trying something different in his efforts to assess spoken English production, then we hope they will also present the teacher with a way of thinking about how the spoken language can be taught. We shall begin with some general conditions on the elicitation of spoken English for assessment and then consider the materials, requirements and scoring procedures which we have developed for this assessment.

Tasks: general conditions

1 The speaker should not be able to see what the listener is doing. Ideally he should be face-to-face with the listener across a table on which there is a low screen. The microphone is placed on the speaker's side of the screen. The speaker knows he is being recorded.
2 The instructions from the examiner should be brief and clear about the requirements of the task. Ideally, students should never perform any of these task types for the first time in a test. They should be made familiar with the format and requirements of the task types through classroom practice.
3 The listener-role should never be taken by the teacher. Ideally, the listener should be another student, preferably of the same level of ability.
4 In a test, the listener should be asked just to follow the speaker's instructions, descriptions etc., and to perform his task without asking questions. He should be strongly discouraged from 'taking over' the transactions and becoming the dominant participant. The listener's role is passive and subordinate in this assessment procedure.

5 The speaker should know that what he says in the performance of one of these tasks is the basis of an assessment procedure. In classroom practice these tasks may be presented as a 'game', in assessment they are to be taken seriously.

Task type A: description

Materials: Two photographs. The speaker has the photograph shown as illustration 1 (p. 150 below). The listener has an almost identical photograph with the addition of a small rubber beside the small pencil at the bottom left of the picture.

Task: The speaker has to describe what is in the photograph as accurately as possible in order that the listener can carry out a task which depends on the description being accurate and clear. The listener has to listen carefully to the description and identify in what way his photograph differs from the one which the speaker is describing.

Requirements: (i) The speaker should identify and distinguish, where necessary, the objects in his photograph. This is a basic requirement which could be satisfied by the speaker providing a list of nouns, or adjectives plus nouns. It is necessary to distinguish between the pencils, pens, rulers and keys shown. Simple distinctions such as *a big pen* and *a small pen* are sufficient. Extract (A1) is a partial transcript of a performance by a speaker who provided such a description. (ii) The speaker should describe the positions of the objects in relation to each other. Extract (A2) is a partial transcript from a speaker who provided some of this required information. Extract (A3) is from a speaker who provided a more detailed description.

(A1)   there's two rulers + a rubber + + a clip + a pen + +

(A2)   two rulers + rubber next to the ruler + + a pen with a top next to the rubber + clip next to the pen + it's to the left + +

(A3)   there are two rulers + there's one ruler thinner than another one + the thin one is on top of the thick ruler + + at the right of the thick ruler there is a rubber + + below the rubber there is a paper clip + + and to the right of the clip there is a pen with a top on it + +

GENERAL REMARKS

The three extracts presented as (A1)–(A3) illustrate different levels of performance in a task of this type. In a sense, all three represent

Assessing spoken language

Scoring matrix

Features	Examples	A1	A2	A3
object (1)	'ruler'	✓	✓	✓
property (1)	'thin', 'light-coloured'			✓
relationship (1–2)	'on top of', 'lying over'			✓
object (2)	'ruler'	✓	✓	✓
property (2)	'thick'			✓
relationship (2–3)	'next to', 'at the right of'		✓	✓
object (3)	'rubber'	✓	✓	✓
relationship (3–4)	'under', 'down from' 'next to'		✓	✓
object (4)	'paper clip'	✓	✓	✓
relationship (4–5)	'to the right of', 'next to'		✓	✓
object (5)	'pen'	✓	✓	✓
property (5)	'with a top', 'big'		✓	✓

reasonable attempts to perform the task required. The teacher, or examiner, might be quite satisfied with the simple listing of objects in (A1) if it was produced by a beginner. However, if all three extracts were produced by members of the same group (of intermediate students, for example), then the teacher is in a position to say that the speaker of (A3) has produced a 'better' performance in terms of required detail. The scoring matrix allows the teacher to quantify in what respects the performance in (A3) is 'better', or more explicit, *in terms of this particular task*.

The scoring matrix can be reduced or expanded, in terms of required detail, according to the level of performance the teacher expects of the student group under consideration. For beginners, it may be sufficient that the identification of objects and their distinguishing properties are included in the description. In that case, the 'relationship' entries need not be included. At the other extreme, the teacher may expect that a particular group of advanced students is capable of producing extremely detailed descriptions and may wish to expand the matrix to include additional detail. Some students produce extremely detailed descriptions of objects as shown in (A4) and of relationships as in (A5).

(A4)   there's two rulers + one on top of the other + the one on the bottom has got inches on the left and on the right is measured in centimetres and millimetres + the ruler on top + on the righthand side is measured in inches and on the left + is measured + centimetres and millimetres ++

(A5)   the large dark ruler is lying straight up and down + and the light ruler is across it + across the top part + at an angle + not straight ++

The scoring matrix we have presented is a basic guideline for teachers wishing to score performances in a task of this type. As in any descriptive task, the competent speaker could produce an extremely lengthy, minutely detailed, account of what is in the photograph. We did not develop this task in order to elicit such extravagant performances. It is a basic level descriptive task, requiring very little preparation and capable of endless variation in terms of objects and arrangements. The scoring matrix is also presented at a basic level.

Given this basic task format and scoring procedure, the teacher can also use the taped performances to check for correct vocabulary, accurate use of grammatical forms such as prepositions, and adequate pronunciation.

This essentially descriptive task can be given an 'instructional' aspect if, instead of the listener looking at another photograph, he has a jumble of objects such as pens, rulers, etc. in front of him which he has to arrange in a layout, following what the speaker tells him to do. Practice in an activity of this sort may lead students such as the speaker of (A1) to develop and use the English language for describing relationships between objects.

To emphasise that this type of task can be used with different objects and the listener's task can take different forms, we offer illustrations 2a, b and c (p. 151 below) as examples of practical materials. The listener has copies of all three sets of vehicles and the speaker a copy of one of the sets. On the basis of the speaker's description of the vehicles in his set, the listener should be able to identify the correct photograph. The difficulty of this task can be manipulated by making the vehicles in each set easily distinguishable, or by including the same vehicles each time, and making only some minor detail on one vehicle different in each photograph. We have found that descriptions (of sets) of objects are generally easier to produce if there are category differences between the objects involved. Thus, a set containing *a bus, a truck* and *a car* makes fewer demands on the speaker's linguistic resources than a set which has *a car with a black roof, a car with a white roof*, and *a car with a small opening on its roof*, for example. There should be no requirement that the speaker be able to identify these vehicles by manufacturer's name (e.g. a Mercedes), only that his chosen description is adequate for the identification of the object concerned. For some listeners, a description such as *a car with a white roof* will be a much more effective description than *a Mercedes*, if that listener is not at all familiar with types of cars.

We shall incorporate the descriptive aspect of this task within the more complex task of 'Giving an eye-witness account', to be illustrated later. We shall also suggest that the listener's task in these examples provides a reasonable starting point for consideration of what material could be used in the assessment of some aspects of listening comprehension.

Task type B: instruction/description

THE DIAGRAM-DRAWING TASK

Materials: The speaker has a diagram of the type shown in illustrations 3 and 4 (pp. 152, 153 below). The listener has a blank sheet of paper, a black pen and a red pen.

Task: The speaker has to instruct the listener how to reproduce the diagram as accurately as possible on his sheet of paper. The listener has to listen carefully and to follow the speaker's instructions.

Requirements: Similar to task type A, in that descriptions of the objects, their properties and the relationships between objects should be included in the instructions. Unlike task type A, the requirements of an instructional task cannot be met by simply listing the objects involved. Also required in this type of task are more specific properties and more specific details of the relationships between elements in the diagram. In this type of task, the listener has substantially less initial knowledge of what is about to be described than in the photograph-prompted description. The speaker is required to take the state of his listener's knowledge (or lack of it) into more careful consideration.

The following two transcribed extracts (of instructions for the diagram shown in illustration 3) are on the accompanying tape.

(B1) (*11*)   the diagram's in the top right of the corner + em approximately + two inches from the top right + downwards + and two inches inwards + there is a large black three + the three is not in the normal three which is curved you know you've got two large sort of bumps stuck together + the top of the three is straight + and the line down is straight like half a Z + then there's the curve at the bottom part of the three + about one inch underneath that there is a + red line + approximately + one and a half inches long + which is directly beneath the three ++ at the right-hand end of where the red stroke ends + and about one inch beneath it + is where there is a black box + this − it is a square I can sort of judge from the rough dimensions ++ the square is approximately + two and a half inches by two and a half inches + em + as I said it is about one inch below + the red line ++ and one in- no about half an

inch below that there is a thick + red line which is exactly
the same length as the bottom side of the square + +

(B2) (*12*)   well in the upper right-hand corner + paper + you sh- you
write eh + a number three in black + + what – underneath
this number + you draw a line + in red + and then
underneath this + you draw a square in black a bigger
square bigger than the number I mean + + and then +
underneath this square you draw a line in red again + + a
line in red + +

Scoring matrix

Features	Examples	(B1)	(B2)
location	'top'	✓	✓
	'right'	✓	✓
object (1)	'(number) three'	✓	✓
properties (1): colour	'black'	✓	✓
size	'large'/'three centimetres'	✓	
relationship (2–1): direction	'underneath'	✓	✓
distance	'one inch'	✓	
object (2)	'line'	✓	✓
properties (2): colour	'in red'	✓	✓
size	'one and a half inches long'	✓	
relationship (3–2): direction	'underneath'/'beneath'	✓	✓
distance	'one inch'	✓	
object (3)	'square'/'box'	✓	✓
properties (3): colour	'black'	✓	✓
size	'two and a half inches'	✓	
relationship (4–3): direction	'underneath'/'below'	✓	✓
distance	'half an inch'	✓	
object (4)	'line'	✓	✓
properties (4): colour	'in red'	✓	✓
size	'two and a half inches'	✓	

GENERAL REMARKS

The speaker of (B2) has consistently ignored the requirement that the
size of objects and the distance between them should be mentioned,
at least approximately. The measurements need not be precise, but
there needs to be some indication to the listener that the object is
approximately two inches rather than ten inches. As we have noted
already, mathematical precision is not a normal requirement in this
type of task. Notice that the speaker of (B1) produces an extended
description of the number three. Clearly we could build into the

scoring matrix a requirement that the *type* of object should be included in the properties to be described. By including 'type' as a property, we could then require, for example, that speakers say whether 'a line' is horizontal, vertical, or diagonal, or straight, or curved, etc. However, we have not found that native speakers performing this task generally include information of this sort. The assumption seems to be that, unless stated otherwise, a line will be horizontal, of regulation thickness, and straight. If such assumptions are a norm for native speakers of English, we would not wish to include those elements as requirements in assessing non-native speakers' performances. The fact that some speakers, as in extract (B1), decide to produce very detailed descriptions of some objects is not provided for in the basic scoring matrix we have illustrated. As we noted in the discussion of task type A, however, the teacher can indeed expand the number of required features in his matrix, if he is confident that the students understand that 'expanded' instructions are required of them.

If the teacher were to give his students practice in performing a task of this type, there are some helpful strategies which could be pointed out. From the speaker's point of view, he may make the organisation of his own task simpler if he begins at the top and gradually works down, as the speakers of (B1) and (B2) did. Beginning with the square, for example, presents more problems in that the speaker has to organise his instructions to cover two different directions. In terms of organisation, a general strategy of describing 'wholes' before 'parts' also seems to make the task easier. Speakers who describe the location and properties of a circle can then quite easily expect the listener to be able to put in a diameter. One speaker, who first described the location and properties of a line, had great difficulty describing how that line became a diameter with a circle round it. For the benefit of the listener, the speaker may be encouraged to say which pen (i.e. which colour) will be required before giving a detailed description of other properties of the object to be drawn. These types of strategies are examples of speech production strategies which do not only relate to the performance of a particular task, but to the organisation of what one wants to say and a consideration of the requirements of listeners in general.

If students develop the ability adequately to instruct their listeners to reproduce diagrams such as that shown in illustration 3, then more complex diagrams can be used to increase the difficulty of the task. As shown in illustration 4, a diagram with an irregular arrangement of objects will necessarily force the speaker to be more explicit and produce more language to get the details correct. Notice that this notion of 'increased difficulty' need not depend on extra vocabulary or additional grammatical structures. It is based on the problems of organising effectively what one has to say for a listener who depends on the effectiveness of the message. It is directly related to difficulties in being 'communicatively effective' in the spoken language.

THE MINCER ASSEMBLY TASK

We have already discussed some aspects of what is required in this task and how it can be scored (pp. 114–16 above). The requirements of the task are similar to those outlined in the diagram-drawing task. The photograph which the speaker works from is shown as illustration 5 (p. 154 below).

The following two extracts (B3) and (B4) are scored for required information in the scoring matrix which follows.

(B3) (*13*) take the large + erm + L-shaped + tube thing ++ and if you turn it so that the widest opening + is facing up at you so that it's flat in your hand + but you've got the wide opening facing up towards you + then if you take the corkscrew bit + erm + and hold that so the n- the end which is notched + which has got a kind of obvious notching so that it fits in + is (? in fact) going downwards + and then if you drop – if you drop it into the wide opening you'll find that it fits in + you might have to screw it down a bit or something + but it should just kind of slot in ++ then + once you've got that fitting in + you take the- the little st- the little cross shape tin- the little small cross shaped bit + which is going to go which is going to fit + on top of the bit you've just fitted into the largest part + and this has got two sides and the two sides aren't the same + because one + is flat + and one is kind of finished off + and if you put it's the side which is flat + it's facing up towards you ++ and whereas the side which looks as if it's been kind of finished off properly is in towards the machine + then on top of the flat kind of little cross piece + you take + the disc with holes + and you just drop that in on top + 'cause there's going to be a bit sticking out + and then when you've done all that + you take the final bit and you just screw it round the edge and it should just hold the whole machinery together ++

(B4) (*14*) okay you take the + the bigger object + and eh + mm + it could be like that + and you put eh + you take also the + long object + yes + and you put it in er with the + the + what can I say I don't know + the longest side + er of the object + you put it inside ++ okay and er then you take er the little object like a- a bit star + and you put it inside

with the flat + side er + up ++ em then you take eh + the
kind of reel with the + yes ++ and you put it in + then
you take the last object and you put it in the correct way

Scoring matrix

Features	(B3)	(B4)
component (1)	√	√
component (2)	√	√
relationship (2–1)	√	√
connecting part of (1)	√	
connecting part of (2)	√	
component (3)	√	√
relationship (3–2)	√	√
connecting part of (3)	√	√
component (4)	√	√
relationship (4–3)	√	√
component (5)	√	√
relationship (5–1)	√	

GENERAL REMARKS

It should be obvious how a task of this type will be particularly
appropriate for assessing the spoken production of students
following some ESP courses. The ability to produce clear and
easy-to-follow instructions on how to do something is not a skill
which even native speakers learn just by learning the words and
structures of their language. It normally requires training and
practice. A crucial aspect of this training must involve making the
speaker aware of what the listener needs to know. A speaker who
'gives up' on trying to provide explicit instructions and says *oh you
should be able to get that bit right yourself* is failing to communicate
effectively. Such a speaker is expecting his listener to do all the work
in the communicative interchange taking place. This 'giving up' is a
noticeable feature of the spoken English of many non-native students
who have had insufficient training in how to use whatever language
they have in a flexible way. Rather than take responsibility for
getting their intended message across, they leave the listener to work
out what might be meant. Unfortunately, the fact that the only
'listener' many non-native students address in English is their English
teacher (sympathetic, knowledgeable and tolerant of partial messages) may have an adverse effect on the student's development of
spoken language skills.

We have also found that straight practice (i.e. repeating the exercise several times) does not lead to significant improvement in performance in this type of task. Given the opportunity to practise, the student typically practises his mistakes. (This observation must be familiar to those teachers who have worked with students using straight language lab drills.) What does seem to 'sensitise' the student to the need to organise his message and make it more explicit is the experience of being the one who is on the receiving end of poor instructions. The experience of not being able to carry out the task with ease seems to make the student realise that the message *does* have to be organised and explicit. Such a finding suggests a strategy which teachers might use in training students to make their spoken English messages more communicatively effective. Once the teacher has identified (via his scoring matrix) some poor performances in instructional tasks – especially the diagram-drawing task – he can play these versions to the whole class and ask them to carry out the listener's task. If the students complain about the instructions being poor, they can be asked to decide what it was, specifically, they needed to know. When they decide that they weren't told the colour of a line, where the line was in relation to the square, or how big the square was, they are in the process of 'teaching themselves' what is required information in a task of this type. Moreover, we often remember better what we work out for ourselves than what some-one else has determined to be the case. Following such a method-ology also puts the teacher in the more effective roles of 'guide', who facilitates learning by organising materials effectively, and 'informant', who provides vocabulary and ways of saying things in English, when the student needs and wants them.

Task type C: story-telling

Materials: The speaker has a cartoon-strip story. The listener has a set of pictures which show scenes or the characters from the story and some from different stories. Alternatively, the speaker watches a short piece of video film (which is action- and not dialogue-centred) and the listener has a set of still photographs, some taken from the scenes of the film and some not.

Task: The speaker has to tell the story so that his listener, who does not know what happened, will be able to carry out a task based on the speaker's clear account. The listener has to identify which scenes or characters fit the account he hears. If the complete set of pictures does not obviously fall into an event sequence, then the listener can be given the set, as a jumble, and asked to put the pictures into the correct sequence, on the basis of the speaker's account.

Requirements: The basic requirement is, of course, that the speaker tell a coherent story, based on the input. The requirements of a story-telling task can be divided into several categories and success in meeting these requirements can be scored separately. We shall illustrate ways of scoring for required detail, referential explicitness and marking change of location. The weighting given to these aspects of story-telling will depend very much on the type of material used, and how the student is asked to use the material. (Note that there is no requirement that the student produce an 'oral composition' of the type which is often sought in 'O' level French oral assessment. The aim is not to produce spoken versions of what would be a good written composition.)

The broadest category is that related to required detail. Scoring for required detail will be based on what story-telling task the student understands he is being asked to provide. If the student has a set of cartoon-strip pictures in front of him throughout his account, and is asked to give a complete and detailed account of what happened, it is reasonable to incorporate a lot of detailed points in the scoring, as exemplified in scoring matrix (1). If the student has watched a film and has to produce his account *from memory*, then the very detailed scoring matrix is inappropriate. This is also the case if the student is asked to provide a summarised or brief version of what happened (actually quite a difficult task in the spoken mode). Scoring matrix (2) can be used for brief or from-memory accounts.

A crucial requirement in story-telling is that the speaker make it clear *who* he is referring to at any point in the story. As we have pointed out already in chapter 2, an event sequence involving a single male character (he) and a single female character (she) and a dog (it) presents few referential problems. However, as we shall illustrate, a simple event sequence involving three female characters forces the speaker to be much more explicit about who he is saying did what. A guide for scoring referential explicitness is presented in matrix (3).

Remembering the principles of analogy and minimal change which operate in interpretation, the speaker should be aware that if he gives a location for a set of events, that location will be taken as constant, unless he indicates a change. We shall briefly illustrate how points of location shift can be identified in a story sequence and how speakers' accounts can be scored for inclusion of this required information.

SCORING FULL ACCOUNTS IN STORY-TELLING

The following extracts (C1)–(C4) are from the beginning of accounts of a cartoon-strip story, partially shown in illustration 6 (p. 155

below). The speakers had the pictures in front of them and were asked to provide a clear and complete account of the story for a listener who did not know the story at all. Points awarded to the different accounts are shown in scoring matrix (1) which follows the extracts. (This scoring procedure is a very lengthy undertaking which we would not advise teachers to perform unless they have a lot of spare time and a specific purpose in mind. We will exemplify the type of detail which can be scored in speakers' introductions to this story, specifically related to the first picture in illustration 6.)

(C1)   it was about a woman and her husband and she was reading a letter

(C2)   the woman was sitting down reading a letter

(C3)   it's about this guy not really enjoying himself with his wife

(C4)   it's about a man and woman sitting in the living room and the woman's reading and the man's getting bored

Scoring matrix (1)

Details	Examples	(C1)	(C2)	C3)	(C4)
location	'living room'				√
male character	'man'/'husband'	√		√	√
activity	'sitting'/'smoking'			√	
state	'bored'			√	√
female character	'woman'	√	√	√	√
activity	'sitting'/'reading'	√	√		√

SCORING SUMMARISED ACCOUNTS IN STORY-TELLING

Extract (C5) is one example produced when students were asked to provide brief versions which covered the main points (from memory) of the story they had seen. Points awarded for this type of account are shown in scoring matrix (2). The research which led to the establishment of the points in this scoring matrix was carried out with native-speaking undergraduates. The elements included here were those which occurred with statistically significant regularity in the undergraduate corpus taken as a whole. Consequently, it may not be an appropriate assessment task (and scoring system) to use with students other than those who are quite advanced. It can, however, be taken by teachers as a guide to the types of elements which form the core of required information in a story-telling task of this type.

(C5) (*15*)   you've got a bored husband + goes off + sneaks off one night to the pub with his friends + ends up at the disco +

slightly drunk + meets fabulous young thing + starts
having an affair + wife discovers them + on the phone to
each other + husband leaves sets up home with the new
girl + then lead the same kind of boredom occurs and the
girls walks off and starts going to the disco on her own

Scoring matrix (2)

Details	(C5)
man (1)	√
woman (2)	
married (1–2)	√
bored (1)	√
go out (1)	√
meet (1–3)	√
girl (3)	√
young (3)	√
leave (1–2)	√
live together (1–3)	√
bored (3)	√
go out (3)	√

SCORING FOR REFERENTIAL EXPLICITNESS

In one of the story sequences we have used and which we partly
described in chapter 2, there is an elderly woman sitting in her
kitchen reading a book. In the story which the elderly woman is
reading, there is a series of events involving a young princess. When
the speaker who is recounting this story-telling task comes to the end
of the section involving the princess, he is required to refer to the
elderly woman again. If scored simply for detail, as in a scoring
procedure like that illustrated as scoring matrix (1), a point will, or
will not, be awarded for mentioning the character. We can suggest
a way of giving the scoring system more discriminating power
when such referential boundaries occur. The justification for this
'weighting' for referential explicitness is provided by an argument
that stories are essentially held together in interpretation by keeping who-did-what quite clear. If it is unclear at some point which
character is being referred to, the interpretation of the story becomes
substantially more difficult to work out. It may not be impossible to
work out which character is probably involved, but the less explicit
the speaker's reference, the more 'work' the listener is required to
carry out. Thus, the scoring system can be made to reflect the level of

explicitness with which the speaker has identified the character involved. Scoring matrix (3) is an illustration of a four-point scale which may be used for scoring how explicitly the speaker identified the elderly woman on her reintroduction into the story sequence. The examples shown in each box to illustrate the different scores contain the introductory mention of the first character (1), the introductory mention of the second character (2), and the reintroduction of the first character (1) again.

Scoring matrix (3)

Score	Type of expression	Noun	Phrase
3	Character distinguished by the noun and by the phrase used	(1) a woman... sitting in her kitchen (2) a princess... in a small room → (1) the woman... in the kitchen	
2	Character only distinguished by the noun	(1) a housewife (2) a girl → (1) the housewife	
1	Character only distinguished by the phrase used	(1) a woman... sitting reading a book (2) a woman... who has long hair → (1) the woman/she... finishes the book	
0	Character not distinguished by the noun nor by the phrase used	(1) a lady... in a kitchen (2) a lady... in her room → (1) the lady/she... is daydreaming	

We suggested earlier that one way to make a task more difficult for a student group who have become adept at coping with simple stories is to increase the 'communicative stress' involved in telling the story. One very specific means of doing this in a story-telling task is to select or create stories which have crucial events involving several same-gender characters. Illustration 7 (p. 156 below) is taken from the middle of one story-telling task we devised. There are three female characters and, although students can get the action clear (someone put a bottle in someone else's bag), they often fail to manipulate their linguistic resources sufficiently well to convey to the listener who exactly each 'someone' was. Extracts (C6) and (C7) are presented as examples. Note that the speaker in (C6) has introduced two of the characters as *a lady* and *another lady* which creates a problem when she subsequently wishes to refer to one character as *the lady*. The identity problem for the listener here is apparently recognised by the speaker of (C6) who goes on to be more specific (if somewhat inelegant) with the clause *who had the bag in the supermarket trolley.* The speaker in (C7) keeps the characters quite distinct as *a lady, her friend, the daughter* with the pronoun (*she*) always used for the last-mentioned character. However, when it comes to describing where the bottle was put by the daughter, the linguistic expression used (*the bag*) is inadequate. The form, with the definite article, suggests that the listener has already been told about this bag and who has it, but it has not been mentioned before. Failure to make it clear which character owns the bag is likely to create interpretation problems for the listener, in that 'the point' of the story depends crucially on *the friend* having the bottle, unknowingly, in her bag.

(C6) (*16*) a lady comes in a + supermarket + and she gets one of the supermarket trolleys and puts her bag in the supermarket trolley + and she wanders along the aisles + and she meets in one of the aisles + another lady + who has also got a supermarket trolley who has a- b- a- a girl + sitting in the trolley + and as they talk + the girl takes from one of the shelves + a bottle + and she puts it in a bag + of the- of the lady + who had the bag in the supermarket trolley + aargh +

(C7) (*17*) there was a lady entering a shop perhaps a supermarket but (- - -) a shop + and then she meets a friend and they begin to talk and this friend of hers has a little + girl perhaps her daughter + the daughter takes a bottle from a shelf and + without them no- realising it + she puts it in the ha- in the bag

SCORING FOR LOCATION SHIFT MARKING

In the story sequence partially shown in illustration 6, there are six points at which a change of scene takes place. These 'scenes' can be listed as: home – bar – disco – restaurant – home again – new house – disco again. Any spoken account of this story should have these scene shifts indicated. In extract (C8), the shift from restaurant to home again is not mentioned by the speaker. One might wonder if the man in the story is telephoning in the restaurant and, if so, how his wife got there.

(C8) he starts talking to the woman + he starts to like her + and (* * *) his wife hears him phoning her + on the phone +

Other speakers are often very careful to make sure that their listeners are following where events are taking place, as in extracts (C9) and (C10).

(C9) the husband's bored + he goes to the mirror + and says to himself I'm going out I'm fed up + *so when he goes out he goes to a bar*

(C10) (*18*)   the man gets so bored that eventually he decides he's going to go out so he dresses himself up in front of a mirror + and off he goes *to the pub* + where he gets a bit drunk + he then wanders off *into a disco* + *when he gets to the disco*

The six points to be awarded for marking location shift can, of course, be incorporated in the full detailed scoring matrix suggested earlier. They may, alternatively, be kept as a separate category which will allow the teacher to check whether a student is consistently neglecting to include this type of information in his account. Indeed, location marking could be taught as an organising strategy for students to use as they proceed through an account of a series of events.

GENERAL REMARKS

We have provided a basis for scoring story-telling tasks in terms of different types of required detail. Other details may be crucial in other stories. For example, in a story involving flashback sequences, it will be necessary for the speaker to mark temporal (as well as locational) shifts. In very complex stories (involving dream sequences perhaps), it will be necessary for the speaker to indicate what is actually happening, and explicitly mark what one character only dreams or imagines is happening. It may be that to make sense of some story sequences, the speaker has to attribute motives (e.g. jealousy, revenge, hate, love) to characters involved.

In addition to factors such as these, teachers may feel that 'telling a story' had additional attributes which we have not even attempted to capture in our scoring system. If qualities such as 'creating suspense', 'involving the listener', and 'illustrating a moral' are to be assessed in a student's story-telling, then our scoring systems will offer no guidance at all. Nor will they be of any help in deciding whether the use of one set of vocabulary items was 'richer' than another. The following two extracts score very similarly in our system, yet the teacher may wish to award additional points for the use of more elaborate vocabulary by the speaker of (C11).

(C11)   there's a car thief operating in the vicinity of this show + probably a circus side show + he's raiding the cars + while this person + Max the Great Escapologist + em escapes from a straitjacket +

(C12)   there was one man and he was in a straitjacket + he was trying to get out + and then another man + breaking into a car + and taking + I think it was a radio +

(We cannot illustrate this particular story here since the elicitation material was a piece of video film.)

We have already stressed our recognition of other features of students' spoken performances which teachers will want to incorporate in their assessments. We think that such assessments will be necessarily subjective, but have a definite place in the overall assessment profile which is compiled for the student. What we have offered here is a means of producing a consistent, fairly objective, basis for assessing those aspects of story-telling which depend on communicating required information and giving the listener a clear account of who-did-what. These skills in using the spoken language effectively are even more important in the next task type we have developed – the eye-witness account.

Task type D: the eye-witness account

Materials: The speaker has a set of photographs of the type shown in illustrations 8 and 9 (pp. 157, 158 below), depicting a sequence of events leading up to a car crash. The listener has a set of photographs, some of which show details of the particular car crash being described and some from another car crash. Alternatively the listener has a road layout design on which he has to draw, in pencil, the locations and movements of the cars involved in the crash being described.

Task: The speaker has to describe the car crash to a listener who has not been at the scene and who needs to know exactly what happened. (The speaker can be asked to give an eye-witness account of the crash, as if to a policeman or insurance investigator.) The listener has to identify the pictures which fit the crash being described, or has to produce a rough diagram of the locations and movements of the cars involved in the crash.

Requirements: The speaker has to distinguish between the cars involved, make it clear which car went where, and which cars actually crashed. We developed the first listener's task (identifying the correct photographs) principally on the basis of the first requirement, that the cars be distinctly identified. The second task is less obviously dependent on descriptions of the cars; it is more important that the sequence of movements be explicit. The listener has the basic road layout as shown in figure 4.5. He is asked to mark out in pencil where the cars are at the start of the description (just roughly, by small boxes or circles) and to show (with arrows) where they moved to.

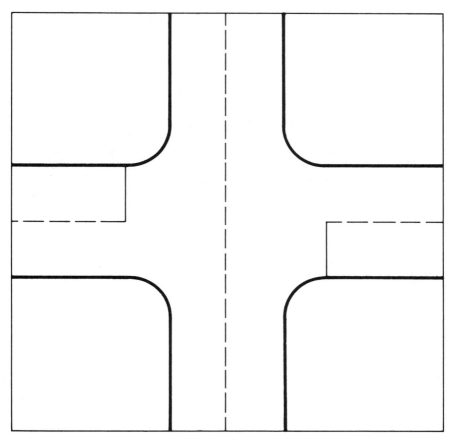

Figure 4.5

The following extracts (D1) and (D2) are accounts of the car crash shown in illustration 8, and are scored for basic required information in the matrix which follows.

(D1) (*19*) it's erm + an intersection of kind of two + a kind of
crossroads + of a minor road going across a major road +
and I was standing there + and there was this erm + kind
of ordinary car + on the minor road + just looking to
come out + on to the big road + and coming down
towards him on the big road was a van + followed by a
lorry + now + just as he started to come out just as the
small car started to come out on to the main road + the
van + no the lorry star-started to overtake the van + not
having seen the fact that another car was coming out + so
as the small car + came right out into the road + the lorry

+ seeing the small car + was unable to come right out +
and overtake the van properly as it had intended + and
ended up slewing into the van in front of it + because there
was no space for it to carry on going round + and because
it couldn't stop in time + it just went straight into the back
+ of the van + and that's what happened.

(D2) (20)   okay we are in a crossroads + and on the right we have a
car + up in this road there is a lorry a little lorry and a bus
+ and so + the bus want to + to + huh + to come and +
the car the car is going to go on the up road + and the bus
wants to + em a- (? avance) + the lorry + and so the bus
when he when it sees the car coming it has to stop and he +
is + (? a scrashed) or in the- in the lorry I don't know if it's
(? a scrashed) or + it bumps on it +

Scoring matrix

Details	(D1)	(D2)
crossroads	✓	✓
car (1)	✓	✓
from right (1)		✓
van/truck (2)	✓	✓
from top/north (2)	✓	
in front (2–3)	✓	
bus/lorry (3)	✓	✓
from top/north (3)	✓	
behind (3–2)	✓	
overtake (3–2)	✓	✓
move out (1)	✓	✓
turn right (1)		
turn right (1)		
crash into (3–2)	✓	✓
drive off/escape (1)		
to blame/cause crash (1)		

The difficulty of this type of task can be increased in several ways.
Whereas in illustration 8, the vehicles are of different types (car,
truck, bus), in illustration 9, they are all cars. Describing the car
crash shown in illustration 9 presents problems in terms of
adequately identifying the vehicles involved at each stage. Two
other obvious aspects of the crash shown in illustration 9 contribute
to the difficulty of the task. There are four (not three) vehicles and
three (not two) of them are involved in the crash. Two extracts of
performances in this task are presented below.

(D3) (21) well + I was standing in the street + at the crossroads and there were two coming – cars coming down each of the lanes + well the em large car I don't really know the sort + em st- didn't bother giving way and just went straight out into the road + em it ploughed into + an oncoming car which in turn hit a third car + and they were just smashed up there + another car just passed them by +

(D4) (22) okay right you've got another intersection + there's a minor road on the right-hand side there are two cars which are going to try and get out on to the main road + one of them is going to try and turn right and that one is just in front of the one which is going to try and turn left so that the one which is trying to turn right is a little bit further out into the middle of the road + coming down the main road + just reaching the intersection + coming down from-from- from the top + is + are two cars + one of which is beginning to ov- to try and overtake the behind- the one behind is trying to overtake + the one in front + so there's four cars altogether + as these two cars are coming along the main road and as the car behind on the main road + is is beginning to overtake + the car in front + the first of the cars from the minor road which is going to try and turn right + is pulling out + to turn right into the intersection + so therefore once you get to the intersection you've got three cars in the middle of the road + three – two cars coming down the main road + one car trying to turn right + and the three of them crash into each other + + the car on the minor road which was trying to turn left + turns left and escapes unhurt

GENERAL REMARKS

The speaker of extract (D3) has given an extremely vague account of the crash. He behaves as if the listener has access to a lot more information than can be expected. For example, there is a reference to *the large car*, but no indication which of the four vehicles this expression is intended to identify. The speaker of (D4) takes some trouble to make it clear which car is doing what (and where) throughout the description. Notice the 'working-out' of the description which eventually arrives at *the one behind is trying to overtake the one in front.* This is a good example of what is a normal feature of native-speaker English production, but which might be treated as 'non-fluent' if heard in a non-native speaker's version of this task.

A scoring matrix, similar to that outlined for (D1) and (D2), can be produced for this more complex version of the car-crash task and extract (D4) would, predictably, score higher than (D3). As we suggested earlier, the listener's task can take forms similar to those suggested for the other tasks we have described. We shall illustrate an alternative format here, which is derived from the 'real-world' requirement of information-representation as found on insurance-claim forms relating to traffic accidents. In illustration 10 (p. 159 below), the listener's task is to put a tick beside the layouts which he thinks are most appropriate to the beginning, middle and end of the speaker's description. If none of the layouts is appropriate, then the 'don't know' box is chosen. We do not suggest that any one listener's task is better than another when the primary interest of the exercise is the elicitation of spoken English. The different forms of listener's tasks do, however, suggest that it may be possible to present students, in *listening comprehension* exercises, with something to do which does not involve writing answers to printed questions.

Task type E: opinion-expressing

This type of task presents difficulties in terms both of developing appropriate elicitation materials and detailed scoring procedures. It may be that this type of task can only be properly assessed subjectively and that, no matter how objective we would like to be, we shall always have difficulty quantifying levels of performance in the expression of attitudes, points of view and justifications for opinions expressed. We shall describe one exercise which we have used with native-speaking students of English, simply as a guideline for what can be a partially successful method of controlled elicitation of opinion-expressing.

We produced a short piece of video film in which a teacher expressed a fairly strong opinion that corporal punishment was necessary in schools to ensure that teachers could do their work and that students would learn. We showed this brief film to high-school students and asked them what they thought about the matter. The range of response was rather disconcerting. Some students had nothing or very little to say, some had quite definite opinions and produced reasons in support and one or two described the scene or recounted what they had just heard. On the basis of our elicited responses, we have produced the rather tentative range of grades shown in the scoring matrix. We are still unsure about the usefulness of this particular method of scoring. We offer it as a suggestion to teachers who are looking for ways to grade spoken production of this type.

The following extracts are representative of the types of response elicited and the scoring matrix which follows provides a basic means of differentiating between them.

(E1)	I don't think it's true
(E2)	I don't agree
(E3)	it's a man sitting behind a desk talking . . .
(E4)	I disagree with him + 'cause there could be other means of punishing people
(E5)	I think it's wrong 'cause + I think the teacher should be able to control the pupils
(E6) (23)	I think it's wrong 'cause I think the teacher should be able to + control the pupils and you know make it + make them realise that they're in charge without having to use violence + I think they should have other means of being able to + control the pupils

Scoring matrix

Extracts	Response-type	Grade
	Silence	D
(E1), (E2) (E3)	opinion expressed or straight description	C
(E4), (E5)	opinion expressed plus reason given	B
(E6)	opinion expressed plus reason given plus support for reason	A

GENERAL REMARKS

The matrix shown above is presented as an outline guide for assessing the content of responses in a task of this sort. It does not have the detailed features of the matrices we presented earlier and may be interpreted much more subjectively. The difficulty encountered in producing an objective scoring structure is a direct reflection of the difficulty in determining the structure of the task. The student who is asked to express an opinion is faced with a substantial task in organisational terms. If the matrix provided above can be taken as a guide for teachers who wish to give their students some 'structure' on which to base the expression of opinion, then it may serve a useful purpose in the training of spoken English production.

4.5 Can listening comprehension be assessed?

In our extended discussion of the task-based elicitation of spoken English for assessment purposes, we have insisted that the performance of the listener in his task should not be taken as the basis for any judgment on how well the speaker has performed. We have tried essentially to isolate the assessment of spoken production from considerations of the student's listening comprehension ability. We have argued, in this chapter, that a listener's task performance may be unreliable for a number of reasons, and, at the end of chapter 3, that we have only very limited understanding of how we could determine what it is that listening comprehension entails. Given these two observations, it would seem that the assessment of listening comprehension is an extremely complex undertaking.

The basic problem seems to involve the fact that there need not be any external evidence that a person has understood what he has heard. Indeed, the normal assumption in native-speaker interaction is that our listeners generally do understand what we say, without *showing* that they understand, except in rather subtle ways (nodding, saying *yes, uhuh*, etc.) occasionally. Yet the occurrence of even these occasional indications must be treated with some caution as evidence of 'understanding'. One participant in a conversation may murmur *uhuh* while another is speaking because he wishes to indicate that he agrees with what he thinks the other is saying. It is possible that his interpretation of what the other is saying could bear a fairly indirect relation to what the other intends him to 'understand'. However, even if we could take the utterance of *yes* or *uhuh* at regular intervals in our listening behaviour as an indication of 'understanding', it would be a rather odd basis for assessing the listening comprehension of foreign learners of English.

Those who have attempted to assess listening comprehension have sought more extended examples of 'reactions' to what has been heard. The traditional type of reaction required is for the student to write answers to some written questions on what he has listened to. If the student produces a set of acceptable answers, it is assumed that this is evidence of his ability to understand spoken English. We should note that it is also some indication of his ability to understand written English and to convey his intended meaning in acceptable written English. In this type of assessment procedure, if the student produces an answer which is considered to be 'wrong', it is scored as a failure in listening comprehension. Interpreting a 'wrong' score in this way is a fairly unreliable procedure. The 'wrongness' of the answer may arise from failure to understand the *written* question or to convey intended meaning in the *written* answer. Alternatively, it may arise from lack of attention to some specific detail in the material listened to or from poor memory for detail.

Recognising these problems which come between the student's listening comprehension ability and the reaction he produces in the comprehension exercise format, many teachers have tried to develop 'purer' listening exercises. That is, they have moved away from the written question-and-answer format and produced grids to be filled in, diagrams to be labelled and other devices which are less dependent on the understanding and production of the written language. There is, inevitably, some written element, but it is kept to a minimum (e.g. single-word headings for columns in the grid, single-word or short-phrase labels for parts of a diagram). Thus, the notion of failure to understand in a listening exercise of this type can be more confidently treated as deriving from the listening activity (and not from reading or writing). The outstanding problem in using this procedure for assessment is that it still has little diagnostic potential. When an 'error' of some sort is identified in the student's reaction to what he has heard, there is little insight gained into what caused the student to produce the error. It could be something as simple as ignorance of a particular vocabulary item, but it could equally be that the student knows the vocabulary item very well, but did not recognise its function within a particular communicative structure.

So far, we have dwelt on the problems of determining, in our assessment procedure, how to interpret the evidence from a student's reaction to what he hears. An additional problem is related to quantifying our interpretations of that evidence. All we can normally say is that the student understood or didn't understand. If we attempt to say that he didn't understand a lot, we should be aware that this lack of understanding may derive from some very small early misunderstanding which had a cumulative effect throughout the student's subsequent performance in the exercise. Alternatively, what is seen as a lot of errors in an exercise may actually be the same simple error repeated over and over again. Nor can we know for sure what the basis of the error is, since we have no access to the processes which brought it about. This last point is in fact the primary reason why we have such great difficulty producing a dependable method of assessing listening comprehension. We may have to come to the rather bleak conclusion that the processes underlying listening comprehension are, in principle, not assessable at all.

If we have to rely on indirect evidence of listening comprehension ability, then we should try to minimise the dependence on other linguistic abilities (e.g. reading and writing) and structure our procedures so that we gain some insight into where a particular

student's comprehension failures occur. The first observation should
lead us to avoid the written question-and-answer format and attempt
to provide some non-verbal exercise for the student to perform. On
the basis of our second observation, this non-verbal exercise should
have some internal structure. In the task-based approach to the
assessment of spoken production, a number of the listener's tasks
which were developed have these required characteristics. That
approach also provides a basis for the selection of material which the
student is to listen to. One other important consideration in a
listening comprehension task, which we stressed in chapter 3, is the
amount and type of speech to be listened to. The spoken input should
be divided into short chunks and it should be produced by a native
speaker naturally performing the spoken task.

The teacher may readily envisage several of the listener's tasks
described in the preceding section as potential listening comprehension exercises. We shall illustrate a simple procedure for taking
some extracts of native-speakers performing the diagram-drawing
task, described on pp. 126–9 above, and using brief chunks in a
very basic listening comprehension task. The student would not be
asked to draw the partial diagrams described, but, instead, would
be asked to indicate with a tick, which one from a set of three drawings best fits the description he hears in each chunk. This qualification
of 'best fits the description' is based on the principle, proposed in
chapter 3, that we do not aim for a precisely *correct* interpretation, but for the *most reasonable* interpretation of what we hear.

The student has the three alternative diagrams shown in exercise 1
in figure 4.6 and hears the chunk of speech transcribed below as
exercise 1 (note that the diagrams reproduced here are reduced
versions of the originals). He selects the diagram which best fits the
description he hears. After a brief pause, he hears the second and
then later the third exercise. In this first exercise, it is the interpretation of *the speaker's use of linguistic expressions* to refer to entities
and properties which is being assessed. In the second, it is the interpretation of the use of linguistic expressions used to describe
the relationships between those entities; and, in the third, the
combination of both entity reference and relationship description.

Note that successful interpretation of the speaker's intended
meaning in exercise 3, for example, requires the listener to identify
the red stroke as the same object as *the red line*; *a black box, a
square, the square* and *it* as referring to one entity; *at the right-hand
end of where the red stroke ends, about one inch beneath it* and
about one inch below as all involved in the expression of the
relationship between one entity and another. Moreover, this
interpretation has to take place, not on the basis of studying written

instructions on the page where the text remains present to the reader, but on the basis of a transient experience of an acoustic blur which flashes by and is gone.

Exercise 1
(24)   well + in the middle draw + black triangle + with the right angle at the bottom right ++ and in the left the bottom left hand + draw a small red two

Exercise 2
(25)   now there's a red line that goes + em maybe about an eighth of an inch + underneath the black line + of the circle + you start at the edge of the circle and work to your left

Exercise 3
(26)   at the right-hand end of where the red stroke ends + and about one inch beneath it + is where there is a black box + this- it is a square I can sort of judge from the rough dimensions ++ the square is approximately + two and a half inches by two and a half inches + em + as I said it is about one inch below + the red line +

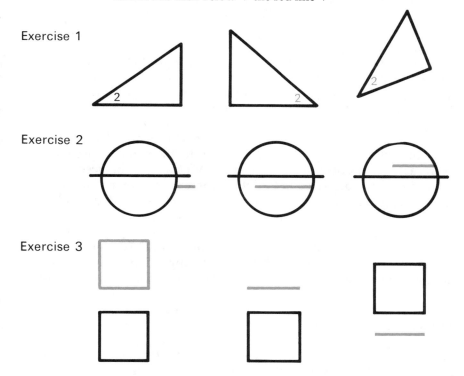

Exercise 1

Exercise 2

Exercise 3

Figure 4.6   Note: grey lines indicate red ▬▬▬

This is, of course, an extremely simple listening task, but we present it as an example of the type of exercise which can be developed from the task-based approach outlined in the earlier sections of this chapter. Other more complex exercises could be developed, on the same principles, using the various task types outlined in section 4.4. We should emphasise that what we have described here is more in the nature of an exercise, which has some diagnostic potential, than an example of an effective assessment instrument for listening comprehension. From an assessment point of view, there are several ways in which this type of exercise is of limited effectiveness. There is a very large input, in terms of preparation of materials, with very little output on the student's part. As a consequence, this type of task may have very limited discriminating power as a test (i.e. it is unlikely that it would provide a very wide range of scores among a student group). As a test, it suffers from the drawbacks of the multi-choice format, in that a very large number of items would be required to reduce the effects of random scoring by a student. Finally, it suffers partially from some of the failings we have noted in almost all commercially available listening comprehension assessment methodologies. It fails to provide us with any genuine insight into the processes by which listeners come to understand what they hear.

We have fairly good evidence in the spoken production tasks we have described for making assessment decisions concerning the speaker's skill in using primarily transactional speech. Descriptions of objects, the relationships between objects, adequate referring expressions, markers of locational shift etc. either *are* or *are not* present in the taped record of the spoken performance. Because this evidence exists, we have been able to present an extended discussion of the assessment of spoken production. We have, in this respect, offered a fairly objective methodology for assessing that aspect of the spoken language which has, in the past, been considered 'difficult' to assess. However, for that aspect which has been considered 'easy' to assess – listening comprehension – we have not been able to offer more than an extended discussion in chapter 3 of the complex problems which those who have produced listening comprehension tests have not even tried to face. The illusion that listening comprehension is 'easy' to teach, as well as to assess, will have to be abandoned before any progress in this area of English teaching can be made. Serious research based on a willingness to question some of the naive assumptions held about the nature of listening comprehension is the most pressing requirement in the study of the spoken language at the present time. We trust that some of the principles and problems we have discussed in the course of this book will stimulate such research and generally lead to a more serious consideration of the primary role which speech has in our use of the English language.

Illustrations

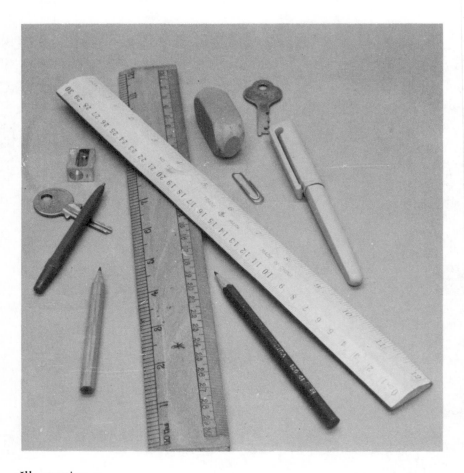

Illustration 1

Illustration 2

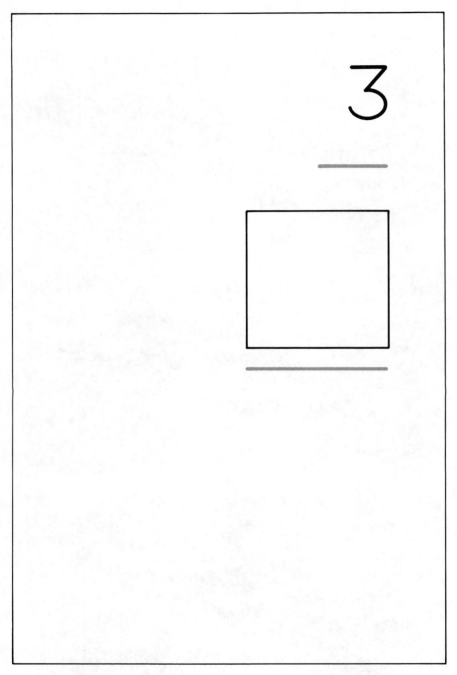

Note: grey lines indicate red ▬▬▬▬▬

Illustration 3

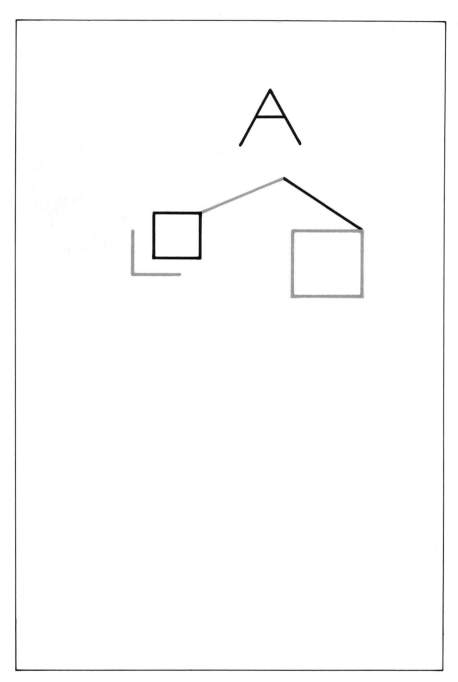

Note: grey lines indicate red ━━━━━

Illustration 4

Illustration 5

Illustration 6

Illustration 7

Illustration 8

157

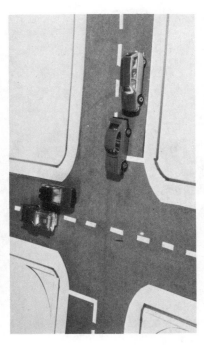

Illustration 9

Beginning of description (Choose one)

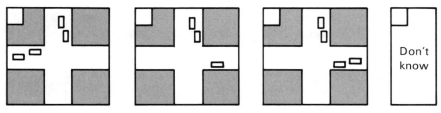

Middle of description (Choose one)

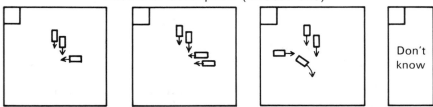

End of description (Choose one)

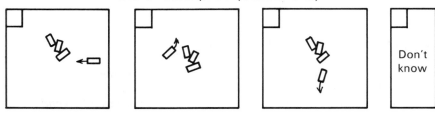

Illustration 10

Bibliography

References

Bartlett, F. C. 1932. *Remembering*. Cambridge University Press
Cicourel, A. 1981. 'Language and the structure of belief in medical communication', in B. Sigurd & J. Svartvik (eds.), *Proceedings of AILA 81, Studia Linguistica*, vol 5
Goody, J. 1977. *The domestication of the savage mind*. Cambridge University Press
Grice, H. P. 1975. 'Logic and conversation', in P. Cole & J. Morgan (eds.), *Syntax and semantics 3: Speech acts*. Academic Press
Heaton, J. B. 1976. *Writing English language tests*. Longman
Labov, W. 1972. *Sociolinguistic patterns*. University of Pennsylvania Press
Lado, R. 1961. *Language testing*. Longmans, Green & Co.
Oller, J. W. 1979. *Language tests at school*. Longman
Popper, K. R. 1963. *Conjectures and refutations*. Routledge & Kegan Paul
Quirk, R., Greenbaum, S., Leech, G. & Svartvik, J. 1972. *A grammar of contemporary English*. Longman
Wilkins, D. 1976. *Notional syllabuses*. Oxford University Press

Some relevant background reading

de Beaugrande, R. 1980. *Text, discourse and process*. Longman
Blundell, L. & Stokes, J. 1981. *Task listening*. Cambridge University Press
Brazil, D., Coulthard, M. & Johns, C. 1980. *Discourse intonation and language teaching*. Longman
Brown, G. 1974. 'Practical phonetics and phonology' in J. P. B. Allen & S. P. Corder (eds.), *Edinburgh course in applied linguistics*, vol 2. Oxford University Press
    1977. *Listening to spoken English*. Longman
    with Currie, K. & Kenworthy, J. 1980. *Questions of intonation*. Croom Helm
    with Yule, G. 1983. *Discourse analysis*. Cambridge University Press
Crystal, D. 1980. 'Neglected grammatical factors in conversational English' in S. Greenbaum, G. Leech, & J. Svartvik (eds.), *Studies in English Linguistics*. Longman
Currie, K. & Yule, G. 1982. 'A return to fundamentals in the teaching of intonation', *IRAL*, 20

Davies, A. 1978. 'Language testing', *Language teaching and linguistics: Abstracts 11*

Donaldson, M. 1978. *Children's minds*. Fontana

Doughty, P., Peirce, J., & Thornton, G. 1971. *Language in use*. Edward Arnold

O'Connor, J. D. 1971. *Phonetics*. Penguin Books

Porter, D. & Roberts, J. 1981. 'Authentic listening activities', *ELT Journal*, 36/1

Stubbs, M. 1981. 'Oracy and educational linguistics: the quality (of the theory) of listening', *First Language*, 2

Thomas, H. 1982. Survey: 'Recent materials for developing listening skills', *ELT Journal*, 36/3

Trudgill, P. 1975. *Accent, dialect and the school*. Edward Arnold

Widdowson, H. G. 1978. *Teaching language as communication*. Oxford University Press

1979. *Explorations in applied linguistics*. Oxford University Press

Index